the
smart
story

the **smart** story

Paul Guinness

Haynes Publishing

First published in 2005

A catalogue record for this book is available
from the British Library

ISBN 1 84425 123 3

Library of Congress catalog card no. 2005921426

Published by Haynes Publishing, Sparkford,
Yeovil, Somerset, BA22 7JJ, UK

Tel: 01963 442030 Fax: 01963 440001
Int. tel: +44 1963 442030
Int. fax: +44 1963 440001
E-mail: sales@haynes.co.uk
Web site: www.haynes.co.uk

Haynes North America, Inc.,
861 Lawrence Drive, Newbury Park,
California 91320, USA

Designed by Richard Parsons

Printed and bound in England by J. H. Haynes &
Co. Ltd, Sparkford

ACKNOWLEDGEMENTS

What has come across so strongly during my time
spent researching and writing this book is the
incredible level of dedication to and affection for
the smart brand all over the world – but particularly in Europe. I can't think of another modern
marque that has such a fanatical following.

With that in mind, it would be impossible to
name here every smart owner and enthusiast that
I have spoken to or who has helped me in some
way with the book.

However, I am particularly indebted to Al
Young, chairman of thesmartclub, for all his
support; innumerable fellow members of both
thesmartclub and funkysmart, who have helped
ensure I've been inundated with photographs and
encouragement; Steve Smith for providing so
much historical data; Phil Egan of midlandsmarts
for helping to arrange photo shoots with various
owners; smart Birmingham for letting me loose
with my camera at their showroom, and finally,
Debbie Hull and Sheena Hamilton of
DaimlerChrysler UK smart for providing information, test vehicles and archive photographs.

On a more personal note, grateful thanks to
Frank Westworth of *Classic Car Mart* magazine for
the laughs and the support, and to Rod Jones,
whose encouragement and countless cups of tea
have been priceless.

The smart scene is unique – and for me to be a
part of it these last few months has been an
absolute joy. Thank you.

PAUL GUINNESS
APRIL 2005

CONTENTS

INTRODUCTION

The announcement of yet another new car in the late 1990s wasn't unusual. Manufacturers the world over were busying themselves with premature launches of 'new-for-the-21st-century' models, desperate to persuade the car-buying public that theirs was a better choice than any of its major rivals.

But the launch of the smart city-coupé was different. Not just because the car itself was radical and brave, but also because it marked the introduction of a whole new brand. For a mass-market design, this was indeed unique.

Let's think about this for a moment. It costs hundreds of millions of pounds to develop a new car, which in itself is a major commitment for any manufacturer. But to develop a new model from scratch and then to launch it as part of a completely new brand, with all that means in terms of advertising spend and persuasive marketing, was courageous in the extreme.

Yet that is what Daimler-Benz, as they were then known, did in 1998 – originally with the help of Swiss watchmaker Swatch, but soon going it alone after the break-up of the partnership. How could all this work? What did Mercedes-Benz and its parent company know about the city car class? Was the world ready for a two-seater commuter car that was more expensive than a good many four-seaters? Would the whole thing end in (very expensive) tears?

From its troubled beginnings in the autumn of 1998, the city-coupé and the then new smart brand name eventually began to prosper. But it could all have been so different. smart had more than its fair share of pre-launch troubles, which subsequently delayed production by several months and added around £100 million to the cost of the project. Then, when original sales expectations had to be heavily revised downwards to prevent major embarrassment by the end of 1999, the future for smart did indeed look dubious.

What is remarkable now is that all such troubles seem a very long time ago. In the years since its launch, the smart brand has truly established itself and, thanks to major product investment, has been transformed into an automotive force to be reckoned with. This is now a company with four

It's one of the youngest motoring marques in Europe – and within six years it went from being a single-model manufacturer to having three very distinct product lines on offer.

◁ The smart roadster manages to offer affordable thrills and the best handling of any small sports car.

▲ The roadster-coupé has been a popular choice with buyers looking for fun and funkiness in a two-seater package.

separate product lines, assembly plants in three countries, a growing customer base and a serious amount of respect and admiration throughout the world. This kind of a turn-around in terms of product design and public perception is simply unprecedented.

But there's more to smart than its products. What really sets these cars apart is the people who spend their own money buying them. No other company's current product range has such a fanatical following; no other manufacturer's latest models boasts such a huge club scene. People love their smarts, and they're not afraid to show it.

In this book, I've tried to give a detailed and entertaining account of the history of smart and the situation it finds itself in today. I have also tried to bring to the fore the human aspect of the marque, talking to countless owners, attending smart events and really getting involved with the whole scene. As I did do, I found myself more impressed than ever with the dedication smart owners feel towards the brand.

Very few companies can boast the levels of customer loyalty that smart enjoys. I hope, by the end of this book, you'll understand why that loyalty exists and why the future of smart is almost guaranteed. This is a unique car manufacturer with a unique range of products – and they are there to be enjoyed.

◁ **Four-seater practicality arrived in the shape of the Smart Forfour, a joint venture with Mitsubishi.**

▷ **That the smart crossblade ended up as a proper production car was simply amazing. Almost as amazing as the car itself, in fact.**

IN THE BEGINNING

So established is the smart brand throughout Europe and other crucial markets these days, that it is easy to forget just what a young company it really is. It was only in April 1994 that what we now know as smart GmbH was officially founded, and it wasn't until July 1998 that production of the two-seater smart city-coupé actually got under way. This is, quite simply, the newest major European motoring marque and is fast proving to be one of the most successful in each market sector it enters.

In many ways, the smart brand seems to have been around for a lot longer. That's obviously an indication of what a major impact it has created in the economy car market of the late 1990s, and continues to do so in these early years of the 21st century. This is even more remarkable when you realise that, for a full five years, smart was basically a single-product company.

The success created by the city-coupé from 1998 wasn't truly built upon until the launch of the all-important roadster and roadster-coupé models in 2003. The debut of production versions of the four-seater forfour the following year consolidated this, and since then there has been an expansion of the brand and its product range which anybody involved in the very early days could only have dreamed of.

GETTING SMALLER

At the start of the 1990s, it was an open secret that Mercedes-Benz was keen to expand its product line-up. The company certainly wasn't short of executive models; it was, after all, an upmarket brand best known for its luxury saloons and sports cars. The success of the 'small' 190 series – launched in 1983 and a major hit for the marque – showed that the expertise was there to open up the brand to a new, less affluent market. Then there was The BMW Factor. Wherever you looked in the Mercedes-Benz line-up in 1990, you would find an equivalent BMW, and with sales of BMWs booming throughout the world, it was

▷ **Guaranteed to turn heads in any city, a smart looks at home in London in 2001.**

▽ **The smart brand is now known around the globe for its innovation and creativity.**

enough to scare Mercedes into some sort of action. After all, the 190 found itself up against the BMW 3-series; the E-class was in direct competition with the 5-series; the S-class saloons had tough competition in the shape of the 7-series, and the SE coupés had to cope with the ageing but still popular 6-series. Wherever Mercedes looked within their range for a 'unique selling point', there was a BMW offering pretty much the same.

One solution was to introduce more 'small' Mercedes-Benz models. The 190 had proved it could be done; in fact, having established itself as Germany's best-selling taxi, it had also shown how a more mainstream model could be introduced without damaging the prestige or reputation of the Three-Pointed Star.

△ The 190 series was the first serious attempt at producing a 'compact' Mercedes-Benz. It went on to be one of the company's best sellers of the 1980s. (Mercedes-Benz)

▽ The world had never seen a Mercedes quite like this before! The all-new A-class was small, innovative and forward-thinking in its design. It showed that the famous Three-Pointed Star could be used on a small hatchback. (Mercedes-Benz)

With 'superminis' getting steadily larger through the 1990s, a new city car class was opening up beneath them. Fiat was one of the first companies to exploit this, launching the diminutive Cinquecento in 1993. (Fiat Auto UK)

What the company needed was an even smaller model that could take the Mercedes brand into new territory. They took a look at the success of the Volkswagen Golf, for example, and realised they wouldn't mind a slice of that particular action – and who could blame them? The debut of the MkIII Golf was just around the corner, a model that was more upmarket than its predecessors and which built upon VW's reputation for solidity, reliability and excellent residuals. Mercedes offered all three characteristics within its own range – but had nothing with which to compete directly with the all-conquering Golf.

Mercedes-Benz did eventually join the Golf set, launching its revolutionary A-class to a shocked public at the end of 1997, before it went on sale throughout most of Europe in the spring of '98. And what a drastic change of direction for the company this was.

The A-class was like no other Mercedes before. Its short, tall styling gave it an almost mini-MPV stance, and its twin-floor design (with the engine situated between the 'sandwich') was groundbreaking in its creation of interior space. Here was a car that was substantially smaller than the Golf, yet offered the kind of spaciousness you'd normally associate with a top-of-the-range S-class. The fact that it was easily affordable by the vast majority of Europe's Golf buyers was the icing on the cake.

Would the creation of a Mercedes-Benz as small as the A-class dilute the company's prestige image? Some fans of the Three-Pointed Star feared it would. The subsequent years – and the launch in 2004 of the second generation A-class – proved otherwise.

CITY CAR THOUGHTS

Even while the A-class was just a glint in Mercedes' corporate eye though, company management started thinking the almost unthinkable. The forthcoming A-class was going to be small, but was there potential for the firm to develop an even tinier model? Could Mercedes actually launch a genuine city car, a commuter special, and get away with it?

It was in January 1993 that Mercedes-Benz officially launched a feasibility study into the development of a city car. But what exactly was their thinking at that early stage? Quite simply, they wanted to revolutionise urban transport, and by spending time looking into their automotive crystal balls, Mercedes predicted that by the end of the Nineties the market for small cars would be drastically different.

The evidence was obvious. By 1993, 'superminis' were steadily getting larger: Fiestas, Polos, Clios and the forthcoming new Punto were all substantially bigger than their various predecessors. And yet, there was only Fiat with its new Cinquecento which was doing anything about

By 1996, Ford had joined the city car bandwagon with its futuristic looking Ka. Positioned below the larger Fiesta, it gave hatchback buyers some extra choice at a very competitive price. (Ford Motor Company)

filling the obvious gap that was being left at the very bottom of the motoring market.

Mercedes predicted in private, that a whole new class of European city cars would be created during the late Nineties, and those in-house experts were proved right. In 1996, along came the Ford Ka to fill the gap left below the Fiesta range and it wouldn't be too long before models like the Volkswagen Lupo, SEAT Arosa and Daewoo Matiz joined the new city car class. By the end of the 20th century, sales of diminutive urban runabouts were booming.

Mercedes-Benz didn't know this for sure in 1993 however. Back then, the company had to rely on its own forecasts and predictions. Even so, it knew that if it were to enjoy any kind of sales success in this forthcoming new sector of the car market, it would have to do things differently. In the same way that the A-class was to be a drastic departure from the Volkswagen Golf in terms of specification and layout, so the new Mercedes city car had to be unique.

The chance to create something almost outrageously different moved up a gear when, on 4 March 1994, a press conference announced to the world a planned joint venture between Mercedes-Benz and what was then SMH – known today as The Swatch Group Ltd. It was exactly the

◁ It was realised early on that a Mercedes-badged city car could cause image problems for the luxury manufacturer. With the help of Swatch, the smart name was finally adopted. (Author)

◁ The principle of using a steel 'skeleton' and cladding it with plastic body panels was decided on at a very early stage. The resulting TRIDION safety cell ended up becoming one of the smart brand's most famous features. (smart UK)

kind of deal that Mercedes had been looking for, but why did it feel the need to jump into bed with another company in the first place?

EARLY PROGRESS

Swatch had already been carrying out research into the feasibility of entering the motoring market when the joint venture was announced. The Swiss watchmaker, famous for its trendy, design-led products, could see a future for a Swatch-badged urban two-seater that set new standards in both funky design and up-to-the-minute technology. It would be like nothing else on the market; no other manufacturer had dared launch a two-seater city car in recent times.

This wasn't dissimilar to the early conclusion that Mercedes' engineers and developers had

come to. Just as the A-class was to be different from anything else at its price, so a sub-A-class Mercedes had to be unique within the city car class. While Mercedes-Benz could boast some of the finest engineering experts amongst its team, what this company did not particularly understand was the 'youth' market. So, if the new city car concept was going to appeal to a new breed of young buyer, Mercedes was probably going to need some kind of outside help in this area. This arrived in the unexpected form of Swatch.

It also meant another important benefit for Mercedes: the newcomer would no longer have to carry the revered Three-Pointed Star. After much consideration, Mercedes just couldn't get away from the notion that a cheap-and-cheerful city car – no matter how technically advanced it was for its size – could have a negative effect on the Mercedes image and could actually disillusion part of the company's loyal customer base.

What they were perhaps less willing to admit in public, was that a Mercedes-badged trendy runabout wouldn't have the same appeal among young buyers as a Swatch-badged product. Mercedes was seen by many 18–30-year-olds as a marque that appealed to older buyers in general, and no matter how accomplished or modern looking a Mercedes city car was, this was perhaps the one sector of the market that wouldn't actually benefit from being part of the prestige maker's line-up. On the other hand, 'Engineering by Mercedes' would make a great marketing tool for a Swatch car…

A month after the joint venture was announced, a new co-owned company was created by Swatch and Mercedes-Benz, registered at Biel in Switzerland and going by the name of Micro Compact Car AG. By the end of 1994, a location had been chosen for what was to be the new company's state-of-the-art production facility: Hambach in France. Things were now moving at a rapid pace.

MAJOR CHANGE

By September 1995, even before construction of the new factory had got under way, Micro Compact Car AG had it first concept vehicle built and ready for reaction. It was, in essence, an early

◁ **From the laying of the foundation stone at the end of 1995 to what you see here – the impressive smartville plant at Hambach, France, was built and made production-ready in a remarkably short space of time. (smart UK)**

example of what was to become the MCC smart city-coupé.

The prototype followed the various ideas that Swatch had been working on prior to the link-up with Mercedes-Benz. The engine was situated at the rear; the cabin was a spacious two-seater, and the structure comprised a steel 'skeleton' with plastic panels attached. Where it differed though, was in its surprisingly conventional engine; Mercedes decreed that a three-cylinder petrol unit should be used in place of the hybrid idea Swatch had been working on.

The newcomer was built and designed like no other economy car of the 1990s. In fact, it was so far ahead of its time in both concept and specification that many motoring pundits began to wonder whether Mercedes-Benz had made a potentially very expensive mistake. Would there really be enough of a market for the MCC to guarantee its future success?

Undeterred, Micro Compact Car AG ploughed on with its development, making use of Mercedes' skilful engineers and Swatch's understanding of successful design and marketing. The foundation stone for the company's new Hambach factory was being laid by the end of 1995, so there was no going back now.

It was at this time, too, that the smart name itself first came into being. Micro Compact Car AG began referring to smart in various announcements, which – as history went on to prove – meant the Swatch name was not going to appear on the vehicle after all. What many had

assumed would be one of the newcomer's biggest marketing ploys – the use of the renowned Swatch branding – wasn't on the agenda any more.

Some motoring historians suggest the name smart was created from 'Swatch Mercedes Art'. It is far more likely though, that consumer research showed it to be a strong, modern brand name for a technologically sophisticated product.

With the benefit of hindsight, of course, this was indeed a sound move. Just a few months after the MCC smart city-coupé finally went into production, Micro Compact Car AG was the subject of a 100 per cent takeover by what was then Daimler-Benz AG. The Swatch involvement was officially at an end and by January 1999, the transfer of all business activities from Biel in Switzerland to Renningen in Germany had taken place. MCC and smart were now wholly part of the Mercedes family.

But why did Swatch pull out of the project at the last moment? There was talk that management at the Swiss watchmaker were disappointed with some aspects of the car – not least its conventional powerplant. It is also possible that, with Swatch originally intending the car to be a cut-price product aimed at young buyers, they felt it had moved too far upmarket. The city-coupé, when launched, was far more expensive than Swatch had ever intended.

With the smart project losing large sums of money in its early stages, maybe Swatch simply got cold feet and wanted to quit before, they

As early as 1996, Europe's motoring press – including Britain's *Car* magazine – was publishing spy photographs of various Mercedes and smart prototypes. (Author)

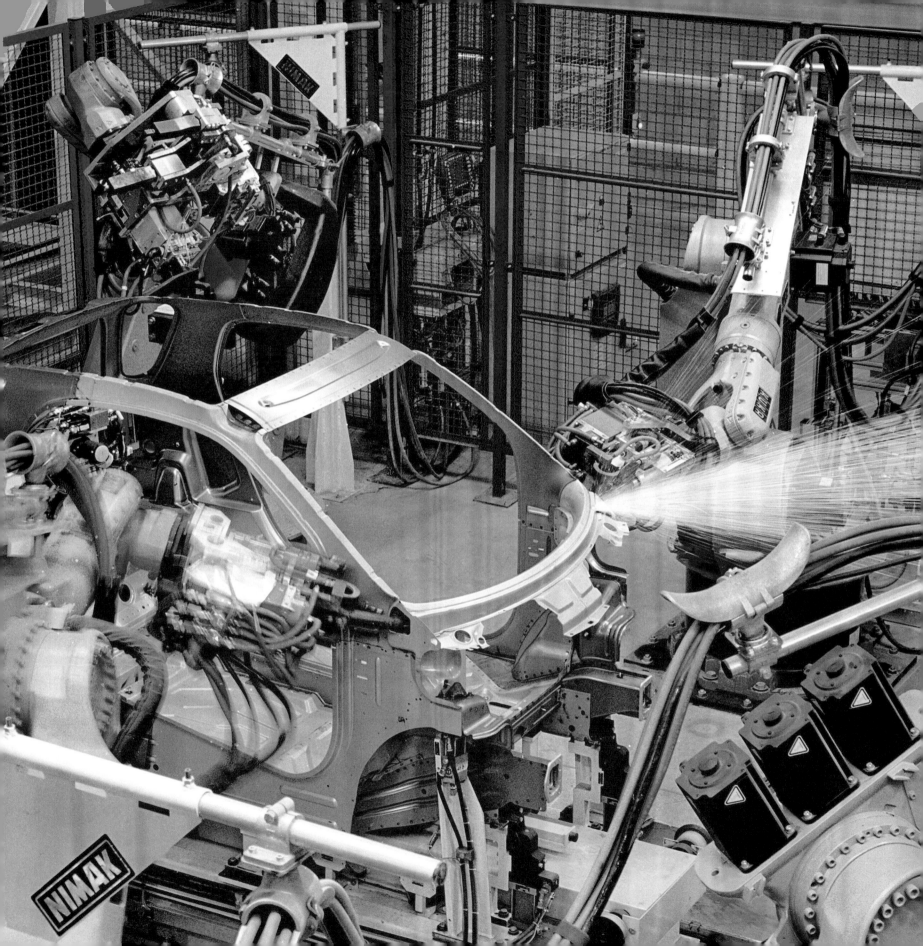

▲ smart GmbH takes its environmental responsibilities very seriously. That's why every TRIDION safety cell is powder coated, a process that creates no solvent emissions or hazardous waste. (smart UK)

◁ The highly automated plant at Hambach is one of the most efficient in Europe. Here the city-coupé's TRIDION safety cell is being welded during construction. (smart UK)

feared, being bled dry by such an expensive and ambitious plan. Either way, it meant Mercedes finally had full control of smart; and in so many ways that must have been a huge relief to all concerned.

PRODUCTION VALUES

From the announcement of the first prototype to the world debut of the MCC smart city-coupé at Frankfurt's IAA exhibition in September 1997 had taken just two years – a remarkably short development period for any new car. It would be a further ten months though, before actual production of the smart would get under way. In fact, the first official examples did not roll off the production line in Hambach until 1 July 1998 – eagerly awaited by potential customers

after so many months of pre-delivery hype and expectation.

But what about the production itself? With a vehicle as unusual as the smart city-coupé, you would be right to assume its production processes would be slightly different from the norm. For a start, smart took environmental issues very seriously, way beyond any legal requirements laid down for the industry, with this applying as much to the production process from day one as it did to the city-coupé itself, as smart officially explained:

'Sky blue and sunset red. smart comes in the brightest colours. Is it all just show? Not at all. Even in the development phase smart GmbH sets great store by the use of eco-friendly parts. The ecological requirements are laid down in a whole string of specifications. And for smart GmbH it is

▲ **Another indication of smart's efficiency is the way the city-coupé's cockpit was designed to be fitted as one single unit. Pre-fabrication away from the main production line speeds up the whole process. (smart UK)**

essential that their system partners take these requirements just as seriously.

'This means that all the parts and components which are delivered are developed and manufactured to consistent ecological criteria. So now the decision to return, dismantle and recycle parts can be taken at some time in the future. Or it can be taken during development. smart GmbH has opted for the latter course, and the ecological requirements form a sound basis here, as well as defining the recyclable materials and specifying the use of recycled synthetics.'

It was all very impressive stuff, and even when it came to issues like the production and finish of the powder-coated TRIDION safety cell, smart was determined to take the lead in terms of efficient, environmentally friendly processes:

'The painting technique used for the TRIDION safety cell is an innovation in the automobile industry worldwide, thus contributing to a maximum in environmental compatibility,' boasted smart. It continued:

'For the first time in the automobile industry, powder-coating is used for the entire vehicle bodywork. Some of the ecological advantages of our powder-coating process are no water consumption, no waste water, no paint sludge and no solvent emissions. The overspray is also reused in an internal materials circuit.'

As well as being one of the ecologically least harmful cars to build, the all-new MCC smart city-coupé was also environmentally sound in long term

usage. Unlike most companies, Micro Compact Car AG put a huge amount of thought into the smart's whole life cycle and the issue of recycling once the car could no longer be used, even setting up its own smart Recycling Centres across Europe. The company was proud of its principles:

'Some parts of the smart see the light of day more than once. Priority is given to the use of synthetics as these can be recycled without difficulty. This is possible because smart GmbH makes eco-friendly choices when it comes to selecting materials. The dashboard is made of polypropylene, for example. So the component of today already contains the material of tomorrow.

'Sustained economy also means accepting responsibility for correctly disposing of residual materials on site. With the introduction of smart Recycling Centres across Europe, we … have succeeded in implementing a comprehensive workshop disposal system in all distribution countries for the very first time.'

It is unusual for a car manufacturer to feature its production processes so much in its pre-launch publicity, but with smart it was a clever ploy. In an age when consumers were becoming increasingly environmentally aware, it was an effective way of gaining some very positive publicity. It presented the smart city-coupé as the car that even the most ecologically minded consumers could buy with a clear conscience, and, just like the design of the actual vehicle, this was a rather useful 'unique selling point'.

PINT-POT PRESTIGE

Onlookers of the time could have been forgiven for thinking Daimler-Benz was rather ambitious in its plans to launch a completely new brand of car on to an unsuspecting public. New models come and go with increasing regularity, but a whole new marque was different altogether.

They needn't have worried. Despite smart being a new and unknown name, its makers knew the brand of Mercedes-Benz was worth its weight in gold when it came to reassuring customers about the city-coupé's credentials. So, while you would never find a Mercedes badge or a Three-Pointed Star anywhere on the smart's bodywork, you only had to lift the engine lid to find

'Engineered by Mercedes-Benz' emblazoned across the rocker cover. If that didn't reassure the great car-buying public, perhaps nothing would.

Happily, it did. Even nowadays, people refer to smarts as being '…built by Mercedes, so they must be reliable.' It's a phrase I've heard countless times over the years, and it was an important boost to the city-coupé's prospects in its early days.

One common misconception about the city-coupé – now known, of course, as the fortwo – was that it was a German car. You can forgive the assumption, bearing in mind the Mercedes parentage. In reality though, it is only the smart's engine, transmission and drivetrain that are built in Germany, at a huge hi-tech factory in Berlin.

Production there started in 1997, and the whole drivetrain package is produced on site before being despatched and shipped to smart's French plant at Hambach.

Soon known as smartville, the massive Hambach set-up was where each and every smart city-coupé really came to life – and it is where the fortwo and roadster ranges are still built to this day. (See the individual photographs in this section for an idea of what goes on.) Needless to say though, it's a hi-tech, highly automated and massively robotised plant that matches just about any car factory in the world for its efficiency and production costs. But then, you wouldn't expect anything less for the world's most technologically advanced city car, would you?

▽ **The city-coupé – now called fortwo – might be built in France, but its three-cylinder engine comes from Germany, engineered by Mercedes-Benz. (smart UK)**

A DIFFICULT BIRTH

That the smart city-coupé took so long to go on sale following its original unveiling in 1997 gave Micro Compact Car AG (MCC) ample time to build up public interest in the project. In turn, this would hopefully ensure a queue of eager customers anxious to get their hands on the smart once it was ready to hit the streets.

More importantly though, it gave MCC and their Mercedes engineers a much-needed opportunity to redesign various aspects of the car which had been severely criticised on pre-production examples. Even before it went on sale, the unsuspecting little smart had been the victim of poor publicity and some disastrous headlines throughout Europe.

In reality, having shown the smart to a fascinated public at Frankfurt in September 1997, MCC wanted to get their baby into production as soon as possible. Daimler-Benz had invested seriously large sums of money in the smart project, and understandably wanted to start generating cashflow. It was widely assumed that sales would commence in the first quarter of 1998.

But then disaster struck – one that would delay the car's on-sale date by six months and cost Mercedes a mighty £100 million in extra development and fault rectification. During some admittedly severe testing, it was discovered that the smart city-coupé simply wasn't as stable at the limit as its designers had anticipated. In fact, when pushed into certain cornering tests at speed, the diminutive car was likely to topple over. For a company still reeling from pre-launch questions about the stability of its A-class range, this simply would not do.

This was a huge embarrassment for the management at both Mercedes and MCC. At the former, it called into question the skills and standards of their own engineers – particularly bad news for a company renowned for its engineering prowess and its prestige image. At the latter it also meant the massively expensive problem of production delays and rushed redesigns.

News reverberated around the world, bringing negative publicity to the whole project, and even before the smart city-coupé went on sale, its production targets were being revised to save any further embarrassment. What had originally been estimated as a 200,000-unit market throughout Europe was soon being downscaled to sales

▶ **By the time the smart city-coupé was unveiled at Frankfurt in 1997, expectations were high. Would this prove to be one of the motor industry's biggest successes of the following year? (smart UK)**

▼ **The TRIDION safety cell looked particularly good when ordered in optional silver, rather than the standard black finish. (smart UK)**

expectations of 100,000 smarts for 1999 – the model's first full year on sale. In fact, at the start of the year, production was stopped completely for a whole two weeks in an effort to reduce stocks and allow demand to catch up with supply. There couldn't have been worse news for all those involved.

MAKING IT BETTER

Remember the bad old days of British Leyland in the 1970s, when underdeveloped new cars would be rushed to market in an effort to prop up sales before being revised and altered a few months down the line? It left owners feeling cheated, and it brought massive warranty claims and serious dissatisfaction from all concerned.

Happily, standards within the motor industry had improved in the subsequent twenty-odd years; so when Mercedes discovered a problem with the smart at the beginning of 1998, it made sure any planned on-sale dates were postponed and it called for major changes – long before any paying customers could get their hands on the machines.

It would be easy to criticise both MCC and its parent group for allowing what was obviously a less-than-perfect design to get almost to production stage. That those in charge then chose to call for major revisions and a much later on-sale date says a lot about how seriously they were taking the issue.

The logic was obvious. It would be better for the smart to receive some negative publicity for a few months prior to its launch in 1998, than for an

⊠ Various stability problems with pre-production examples meant a serious – and very costly – delay for the city-coupé. This innovative newcomer couldn't have got off to a worse start. (smart UK)

By the time the little smart finally went on sale in October 1998, it offered a drastically improved driving experience. Shown here is a 2000 model. (Author)

the back resulted in bigger wheelarches than the original stylists had ever intended, although the overall effect of this was very pleasing, giving the new city-coupé more of a sporty look and, most onlookers agreed, a bit more 'attitude'. Interestingly, the Japanese-market city-coupés that would eventually be produced were the only ones to retain the previous wheel and tyre set-up, as the wider rears contravened the strict K-car class dimension rules for that market.

These alterations were accompanied by a basic suspension upgrade, retaining the original front leaf springs and the coil-sprung de Dion rear set-up but firmed-up to ensure less body roll. Inevitably, this reduced the ride quality of the production smart compared with earlier proto-types, but it was seen as a necessary change if the

The rear wheelarches of the production city-coupés were larger than first anticipated, to accommodate wider wheels and tyres. Stability and aesthetics were both improved as a result. (Author)

WHAT SMART SAID: CITY-COUPÉ

'Half the size of most other cars (2,500mm long and 1,510mm wide), the smart is a high profile example of automotive innovation. It is designed to revolutionise personal transportation in the urban environment and combines safety and fuel economy at a competitive price.'

unmodified car to go on sale and receive the same kind of damning publicity for a lot, lot longer. Before any buyers were allowed to get behind the wheel, the smart had to be absolutely right. Credit should therefore go to the management at Daimler-Benz for making such an obvious but courageous decision.

Indeed, by the time Europe's first smart buyers were taking to the roads in October 1998, following the start of 'proper' production on 1 July that year, the city-coupé was a very different driving experience from those pre-production examples. The engineers had taken the problems very much to heart, transforming the smart into a top-handling little funster with a youthful new character.

Much of the change was due to alterations in wheel and tyre sizes, the fronts being made narrower and the rears wider to make the car understeer in extreme conditions – certainly preferable to ending up on its side. The change at

car was to remain on four wheels. At this stage, smarts came with what the company called the TRUST suspension set-up, rather than the TRUST-PLUS that arrived later – complete with electronic traction and stability control.

This helped to enhance the smart's ever-improving agility still further, TRUST-PLUS operating automatically when necessary. By cutting power or momentarily applying the brakes to restore control in any handling emergency, it succeeded in transforming the city-coupé into far more of an idiot-proof experience.

The downside of such changes was the deterioration in ride quality mentioned earlier, along with a degree of understeer and a general lack of 'feel' from the steering itself. Britain's *Autocar* magazine, testing an unofficially imported city-coupé passion in April 1999, reported: 'All this makes the smart unfailingly safe. But that still doesn't excuse the fidgety ride quality and the suspension's inability to deal effectively with speed humps.'

Both MCC and Mercedes were happy with such appraisals though. After all the furore over the pre-production smart's stability problems, they could endure a certain amount of criticism of the city-coupé's hard ride if it meant phrases like 'unfailingly safe' being used in independent road tests. The smart city-coupé was, at last, the car it always should have been.

◁ With all the changes that had been made, no wonder motoring magazines were using phrases like: '...unfailingly safe' in their road tests. A major transformation had been achieved. (smart UK)

In the same way that the Mercedes-Benz A-class ended up being successfully re-engineered to combat criticisms of instability, so the all important smart had been similarly transformed. Following the problems with the A-class, Mercedes employed the services of tennis star Boris Becker for a series of advertisements in Germany, quoting him as saying: 'I learned more from my defeats than from my victories.' The same could easily have been said of the smart city-coupé.

SAFETY FIRST

It was unfortunate for smart in those early months that any publicity the city-coupé received tended to focus on the controversy over its handling. It was almost as though the rest of the newcomer's amazing design was being ignored, but not for long. With the handling and safety aspects of the car finally sorted, potential buyers started looking a little deeper – and were amazed at just how different from the norm the city-coupé was, both in its design and its construction techniques.

Few onlookers nowadays don't already know about smart's TRIDION safety cell, the powder-coated steel structure that provides the two-seater with its integral strength and the skeleton from which its thermoplastic 'skin' hangs. Back in 1998 though, this was headline-grabbing stuff, even though the main reason for noticing it was because Mercedes had – rather cleverly – made TRIDION an essential part of the car's styling.

Throughout the 1990s, safety had become a saleable issue. Manufacturers were just waking up to the fact that it was a useful marketing tool – and Mercedes knew this. They also knew that any car measuring just 2.5 metres in length would immediately have its safety and crash resistance called into question. How could such a tiny car possibly be safe in an accident?

△ Making a car as small as the city-coupé as safe as possible was no mean feat. smart's clever use of the TRIDION safety cell though, was headline-grabbing stuff. (smart UK)

The answer lay in the clever design of TRIDION, but simply talking about TRIDION wouldn't guarantee public awareness of it. The logical answer then, was to make it one of the city-coupé's most noticeable features by leaving it exposed rather than hidden beneath the plastic panelwork. Obviously, there's a lot more steel in a city-coupé (or fortwo, as it is now known) than you can see at a glance, but the primary aim of getting TRIDION's main shape – sweeping under the doors, up the rear pillar and back towards the front of the car – on full show was achieved superbly. The whole effect was made even more dramatic when TRIDION was ordered with the optional silver finish rather than the standard black.

Thanks largely to the clever TRIDION design, the smart city-coupé soon found itself receiving praise in various European crash tests. The best-known independent tests – Euro NCAP – saw the city-coupé doing well by the standards of 1998, with a front and side impact rating of three out of five, and a pedestrian test rating of two out of four. Euro NCAP praised the smart for being '...very strong and stiff in frontal impact', although in a side impact test '...the dummy's head hit the rail above the door'. Always keen to address any criticisms, smart ensured the city-coupé was available with optional side airbags from April 1999, as well as a revised 'cant rail' head pad and side airbags package from June 2000.

The safety of the smart city-coupé wasn't confined to its TRIDION safety cell and range of airbags, though. Standard equipment from day one included ABS brakes, the traction and stability control systems, small crumple zones built into the plastic panelwork and, of course, a user-friendly semi-auto transmission which – when in fully automatic mode – certainly helped to reduce driver distractions on busy city streets. All of which

◁ Beneath the skin, the smart's three-cylinder engine and six-speed sequential transmission made a unique combination in the city car class. (smart UK)

The pulse and passion models both had a healthier 54bhp (at 5,250rpm) and 59lb ft of torque (at just 3,000rpm). Britain's *Autocar* magazine, in their city-coupé passion road test of April 1999, confirmed the newcomer's electronically limited top speed of 84mph (135km/h), with the 0-60mph (96km/h) 'sprint' taking a rather languid 17.6 seconds – although, in fairness, any city-coupé has always felt much faster than this in day-to-day use.

Transmission on all models at launch was, of course, smart's newly developed six-speed sequential design, comprising three forward gears operated through two final drive ratios. It could be used in fully automatic mode (called Softouch by smart, for reasons best known to themselves) or as a semi-auto with automatic clutch and sequential gearchanges. It was revolutionary for any small car, and enthusiastic owners seemed to enjoy rocking the stubby gearstick backwards and

was great on paper, but would the average small car buyer of Europe and beyond take to the whole driving experience?

BENEATH THE BODY

Fortunately for smart, the city-coupé never was aimed at the average car buyer. While most small-car customers were snapping up four-cylinder, front-wheel-drive conventional hatchbacks, along came smart with its rear-mounted three-cylinder turbocharged engine, rear-wheel drive and two-seater layout.

By the late 1990s though, there was a significant minority of buyers who were indeed willing to sample something a bit unusual. While the smart city-coupé never pretended to be the fastest kid on the block, its unique driving style and idiosyncratic design would surely guarantee it more than a few friends?

From launch, the city-coupé came in three versions: pure, pulse and passion. All shared the same 599cc three-pot motor, albeit available in two different states of tune. Power for the entry-level pure totalled a mere 45bhp, although at least the smart's lightweight design and – finally – sharp handling meant rapid progress could be made even on twisty country roads.

▽ More expensive than Swatch had originally envisaged, the city-coupé nevertheless offered good value when its various technological innovations were taken into account. (Author)

▲ The city-coupé impressed many with its amazingly spacious interior, plus easy access via the two enormous doors. (smart UK)

forwards to change up and down the gearbox, each change taking a reasonable 0.4 seconds.

Driven as a fully automatic, the early smart city-coupé never seemed quite as happy. Many testers criticised the set-up for continually hunting for the right gear, and being very hesitant about selecting the ideal one; it could make for jerky

WHAT THE PRESS SAID: CITY-COUPÉ

'The smart is in full production after what seems like years of development. This two-seat city car was jointly developed by Mercedes and Swatch, although the German manufacturer took over the whole show during the final stages. The rear-mounted 600cc turbocharged engine is available in either 45bhp or 54bhp form. Neither is going to set the tarmac alight, but there is sufficient power to provide lively performance and the car is both intriguing and fun to drive. Amazingly, there is a six-speed semi-automatic Tiptronic-style transmission – just like in a Porsche.'

Daily Express World Car Guide 2001 (UK)

and frustrating progress, leading many owners to stick with the far-more-fun sequential setting at all times.

Although the smart city-coupé was far more expensive at launch than Swatch had ever intended, few buyers could complain about its standard equipment. As well as all the safety wares already mentioned, the top-of-the-range passion even offered air conditioning and alloy wheels as part of its package.

Even so, some pundits still criticised the new smart for its higher-than-expected pricing policy. Could this really be considered a cheap-and-cheerful new product? No, of course not, but it was certainly a well designed, ultra chic form of urban transport with a higher level of technological and electronic wizardry than just about any other small car of the time. This alone made it stand out in an overcrowded and frankly dull small-car market.

OUT ON THE ROAD

The emphasis, of course, was on the word 'urban'. That's what the car was originally designed and created for, after all. Even so, smart owners were soon realising just what a useable little machine it was in other situations. Anybody

▷ By the standards of 1998, both the smart's dashboard style and the imaginative use of colour were funky in the extreme. (smart UK)

who has ever been overtaken on a motorway or an autobahn by a smart city-coupé being driven flat-out will already know this is the case!

First-time drivers of the smart tend to be pleasantly surprised once they are on board. The doors are huge in comparison with the length of the car, which make getting in and out incredibly easy, and once in position, most people are astonished at the amount of head and leg room. There really is space for the driver and passenger to stretch out, even if both are well over six feet in height.

Visibility, too, is worthy of praise. The city-coupé is a very 'glassy' design anyway, and with a high-up driving position more reminiscent of a small MPV than a city car, few people feel vulnerable or have difficulty in manoeuvring the city-coupé into even the most ludicrously small parking spaces.

This is where the smart really excels. Roadside gaps that would normally only be filled by the odd motorbike are suddenly available to smart drivers parking their city-coupés nose-to-kerb. Even nowadays, passers-by stop and stare in amusement as yet another smart driver manoeuvres into a bike-size space.

While highly manoeuvrable, the early smart's lack of power steering surprised some buyers, particularly as there was a whole host of other more expensive goodies on board. At anything above parking speed though, the steering felt light and easy, even if it did lack 'feel' on the motorway.

Owners who worked their all-alloy 599cc three-cylinder six-valve engines particularly hard

WHAT THE PRESS SAID: CITY-COUPÉ

'Finally, Mercedes has caught on to the fact that Brits seem capable of taking the smart seriously. Small and moderately ridiculous looking it might be, but it's well built, spacious for two, and a hoot to drive once you've adapted to the squeally understeer. The perfect second car?'

Car magazine (UK), December 2001

◁ The city-coupé was obviously most at home in an urban or city environment, astonishing passers-by with its ability to squeeze into the tightest parking spaces. (smart UK)

were in for a noisier experience than most – although the engine note and noise levels certainly compared favourably with the 'three-pots' fitted in the Vauxhall/Opel Corsa in more recent times. In fact, the engineers at Mercedes deserve praise for developing what must be one of the world's best three-cylinder engines – despite it being one of the smallest.

Making use of the engine's extensive rev range via the sequential semi-automatic gearbox, it was possible to extract the most get-up-and-go from your city-coupé with relative ease. Inevitably though, you paid the price at the pumps. While official UK figures of the time claimed a city-coupé passion could return up to 48.7mpg on the 'Urban' cycle and a massive 67.3mpg using the 'Combined' calculation, *Autocar* magazine managed a rather less impressive 32.9mpg overall. This did include lots of performance testing though, and wasn't necessarily representative of what a smart buyer might achieve in daily use.

Whether in city conditions or out on the open road, production versions of the city-coupé won friends thanks to their improved handling and sheer peppiness. These were eager little machines, always willing to be pushed harder and harder in an effort to keep ahead of the bigger-engined vehicles around them. The firm ride seemed to encourage enthusiastic driving, as well as reducing body roll at the limit. That didn't stop *Autocar* magazine from issuing the odd criticism though: 'Body roll is negligible, but grip from the skinny 135/70 R15 front tyres is poor, the nose running quite wide even at modest speeds.' Not everyone, it seems, had fallen instantly in love with the little smart.

WAIT AND SEE?

Following the handling debacle of the pre-production examples, the delayed launch and the less-than-ecstatic response of the European motoring press, the management at MCC held their corporate breath to see how sales of their all-new city car would fare. As October 1998 arrived, those customers in Belgium, Germany, France, Italy, Luxemburg, Austria, Switzerland, Spain and The Netherlands who had placed orders since July that year finally started taking delivery.

WHAT THE PRESS SAID: CITY-COUPÉ PASSION

'Meet the bastard son of Mercedes-Benz, the MCC smart. As the offspring of a brief and torrid affair between Mercedes-Benz and Swiss watchmaker Swatch, the Micro Compact Car smart at one time looked set to revolutionise the city car concept. With the chic of a fashionable watchmaker behind it and the engineering might of a Stuttgart star, it seemed certain to succeed.'

Autocar magazine (UK), April 1999

Their response was crucial; the future of smart lay in the hands of the car-buying public of nine European countries.

Less than one month after European deliveries of the smart began, of course, Swatch pulled out and Mercedes-Benz was in charge of the whole project. Did the accountants at Swatch breathe a sigh of relief in November 1998, once they were no longer involved? Quite likely. Meanwhile, with the massive and unprecedented merger of automotive giants Daimler-Benz AG and the Chrysler Corporation now official – leading to the formation of DaimlerChrysler – there was even more pressure on the long awaited smart city-coupé to excel in its debut markets.

STEADY DEVELOPMENT

Even in an era when takeovers, mergers and collaborations have become an integral part of the world's motor industry, few experts could have predicted the coming together of Daimler-Benz and Chrysler. It was hard to imagine two more disparate motoring giants. One, the star of Stuttgart, was a renowned European manufacturer of executive saloons and luxury sports cars. The other, an all-American group with a varied history of financial highs and lows, was more used to building SUVs and trucks.

Sometimes, as with human relationships, opposites really do attract in the motor industry. Nevertheless, pessimistic commentators were soon predicting political fallout in this instance, as well as untold problems caused by a bewildering array of different models and various replacement programmes. It would, they claimed, take at least a decade for the new DaimlerChrysler giant to fully get to grips with the challenges ahead and to make any real benefits from component-sharing across the different brands.

Several years on, of course, the relationship is generally working well – and just look at the incredible variety of motoring brands now together under the DaimlerChrysler corporate umbrella. Mercedes-Benz, Maybach and smart make up the European car building side, while in the States there's Chrysler, Jeep and Dodge representing the car, SUV and pick-up markets. Commercial vehicles are also a big part of DaimlerChrysler, thanks to ownership of Setra, Freightliner, Sterling, Western Star and Fuso, as well as the massively successful Mercedes-Benz truck line-up. It's an impressive list of brands; smart, it seems, is in good company.

EARLY PROGRESS

So would the creation of the new DaimlerChrysler empire cause any particular change of direction for smart? In essence, no. But it certainly put extra pressure on the brand to achieve respectable sales early on if it was to be guaranteed a long-term future.

With DaimlerChrysler in full control, smart's business activities were formally transferred from Biel in Switzerland to Renningen in Germany on 1 January 1999. The company name was also subtly

▼ **How's this for a fun and funky wind-in-your-hair experience? The announcement of the cabrio in March 2000 won smart many new friends. (smart UK)**

changed to Micro Compact Car smart GmbH to differentiate it from its 'predecessor'. But 1999 still looked like being a tough year for the marque.

It was inevitable that once deliveries of the first smart city-coupés got under way, the controversy over the earlier handling difficulties would start to fade. It's true that both consumers and the motoring press have frustratingly long memories at times. However, it is equally true that, with a product as distinct and different as the smart, onlookers would become more interested in the looks, design and driving appeal of the car than in its earlier pre-launch difficulties. At least, that's what smart – the company – was hoping.

To an extent, that is indeed what happened.

Even so, early sales predictions for smart had to be drastically downscaled in order to prevent major embarrassment at the end of the year. In fact, in December 1999, smart had quite a celebration when the 100,000th city-coupé rolled off the production line in Hambach; it was a way of getting some much-needed positive publicity for their little city car. Understandably, they were less keen to admit that the original sales target was 200,000 cars a year.

Still, at least the smart project had made it through the city-coupé's first full year on sale without any other disasters or controversies, which in itself was worthy of celebration. Surely things could only get easier from now on?

◁ As time went on, memories of the earlier handling debacle started to fade. Even so, sales forecasts for the city-coupé were being scaled down… just in case. (smart UK)

They could get easier, but only if smart focussed on improving the basic product and introducing new variations on the same theme as soon as possible. The latter happened at around the same time that the 100,000th smart was built, in December 1999: the introduction of the diesel-powered smart cdi.

It was easy for industry pundits to question the need for a diesel smart. British onlookers in particular, commenting from a market where sales of diesel cars were still very much in the minority at the end of the 1990s, suggested an oil-burning smart would be far too slow to appeal

◁ Petrol versus diesel? The latter offered the advantages of astonishing fuel economy, although it lacked some of the performance of the petrol-powered versions. (Author)

△ Expansion of the smart range meant the introduction of the diesel-powered cdi model for the 2000 model year. It has remained a permanent member of the line-up ever since, but not in the UK. (Author)

WHAT THE PRESS SAID: CITY-COUPÉ

'For: Bucket-loads of character; very practical for driving and parking in the city; roomy inside for two; excellent economy. Against: Painfully slow; too expensive; left-hand drive only; unassisted steering can be heavy; six-ratio gearbox not great. Verdict: Novel; practical little city car.'

What Car? magazine (UK), November 2000

to young buyers and might have only a moderate improvement in fuel economy in its favour. smart had done their research however, and they reckoned sales of diesel-powered cars were going to escalate at an unprecedented rate in the early years of the 21st century.

They were right, of course. With deliveries of the new smart cdi building by January 2000, the company was ready and waiting for any major change in buyers' demands and preferences.

The smart cdi itself was an intriguing little car. It was mechanically all but identical to any other city-coupé apart from its use of a 799cc common-rail direct-injection three-cylinder powerplant. And the biggest headline boast? This was – and still is – the world's smallest production diesel engine.

Developed from the existing three-cylinder, six-valve engine, the diesel version needed its extra 200cc to keep power output at a reasonable level – in this case, 40bhp compared with the city-coupé pure's 45bhp. Top speed was still artificially limited to 84mph (135km/h), but the 0–100km/h (0–62mph) time had increased to a yawning 20.8 seconds. As with other city-coupés though, the cdi felt faster than any such figures might suggest.

Where the cdi scored, of course, was in its fuel consumption. Early owners were reporting average figures in the region of 70mpg-plus – which, for a car that tended to spend most of its time in stop-start urban conditions, was truly impressive. It was certainly a far more economical vehicle than any petrol-engined smart had been up until now.

Just as important for many buyers was the cdi's impressive emissions figure of only 90 grams of CO_2 per kilometre, an achievement that – according to smart – made the world's smallest diesel engine '…a real contribution to climate protection.' That fact alone would be enough to win it many fans.

Perhaps inevitably though, the cdi wasn't quite as much fun to drive as any other city-coupé – and in a market where fun and fashion are the two keywords, this was a bit of a problem. The cdi didn't have the petrol model's rev-happy nature, its eager get-up-and-go and its entertaining exhaust note; it sounded ever so slightly harsh by comparison.

Even so, the cdi was a valuable new member of the smart family. It filled an obvious gap in the city-coupé line-up, and it was bound to appeal to a significant number of buyers for whom only diesel power would do. It made sense – even though 'making sense' wasn't necessarily smart's biggest marketing asset.

OFF WITH THE ROOF!

The other big news as far as the early years of the city-coupé were concerned was the introduction of an eagerly awaited smart cabrio in March 2000. As with the rest of the range, sales were initially restricted to Belgium, Germany, France, Italy, Luxemburg, Austria, Switzerland, Spain and The Netherlands. How would such a fully European market take to the idea of a minuscule soft-top?

Rather well, is the obvious answer. Despite the fact that, on paper, a smart cabrio seemed to make more sense on the sun-soaked roads of southern Spain than in the snow-capped mountains of Switzerland, sales of the newcomer got off to a healthy start in just about every market – and continued to build through the rest of that year.

The idea behind the smart cabrio was simple – as were the engineering changes. Because of the city-coupé's unusual design and construction method, using the TRIDION safety cell to give the car its strength and rigidity, the idea of removing the roof was remarkably straightforward. The rear

▽ **With the hood lowered or raised, the city-cabrio was a good-looking addition to the smart line-up. The numeric blue body panels of this example suit it particularly well. (smart UK)**

section of TRIDION acted as an in-built roll bar, while the plastic roof and rear window areas were replaced with an electrically folding fabric roof.

It was possibly the easiest cabriolet 'conversion' ever carried out by a major manufacturer. Having said that, smart took time and money to ensure the design was spot-on from day one. The hood had to glide effortlessly, as well as being completely watertight when shut; noise levels had to be roughly in line with those of the hardtop city-coupé; and the whole car had to retain the feeling of quality and robustness for which the city-coupé had already been praised.

To give the cabrio an appearance distinct from the city-coupé, it also featured new-look front lights – now known as the 'peanut style' due to their unusual shape. Most buyers thought they

like any new car though, it wasn't perfect. smart knew it had to continue evolving the city-coupé if it was to convince larger numbers of potential buyers to take the plunge and join the smart set.

In fact, during the city-coupé's first four years of life, it found itself on the receiving end of improvements and enhancements on an annual basis. This helped to transform the model into a far more user-friendly and sophisticated product than those earlier examples.

Comparing the specification of a 2003-model city-coupé with one from four years earlier really brings this home. Most significant change was the enlargement of the three-cylinder petrol engine, up from 599cc to 698cc thanks to a bigger bore and longer stroke. This resulted in the entry-level pure derivative having a power output of 50bhp, with the passion boosted to 61bhp.

looked great. So did smart, it seems, as by 2002, 'peanut' headlamps had become standard on all cabrios and city-coupés as part of a mini-facelift that year.

Fortunately for the car-buying public, smart did an excellent job of developing the smart cabrio. Europe's motoring press was just as pleased as those smart fans who had already fallen in love with the newcomer. 'This could be a red-letter day for sun lovers,' enthused Britain's *Auto Express* magazine when its testers got behind the wheel of a cabrio for the first time. They went on: 'smart has delivered a different way of getting wind in your hair with a soft-top that can claim to be the cheapest new cabriolet currently available…' They were impressed.

This was indeed the cheapest proper convertible on sale in Europe, despite costing up to 30 per cent more than the equivalent city-coupé, depending on which trim level the buyer opted for. smart had a trendy new product on its hands that, for once, wasn't criticised for being overpriced. Things were definitely looking up.

IMPROVEMENT CITY

Even so, smart couldn't afford to become complacent. By the time the city-coupé finally went on sale in 1998, it was an accomplished design and a significant improvement over earlier prototypes;

The latter meant 1.3 seconds being shaved off the all-important 0–60mph time, and because the engine wasn't having to work as hard as before (as well as being aided by an improved electronic management system), official figures showed an average fuel consumption of up to 60mpg with careful driving.

Just as important as the boost in power was the

15 per cent increase in torque levels below 3,000rpm. It meant a broader delivery of power, a less stressful driving experience and more relaxing journeys. It also meant fewer gear changes at lower speeds or when tackling steep inclines – although, fortunately the gearchange itself had been completely transformed.

Read any contemporary road tests of an early city-coupé and you'll find one of the most criticised areas was the transmission. In fully automatic mode it was slow and ponderous, and as a semi-auto sequential set-up it was equally jerky. smart took this to heart, and in 2002 equipped the city-coupé with a drastically modified transmission.

When used in fully automatic mode, the new set-up was much quicker and smoother than before; it even boasted a good old-fashioned kickdown feature, something which previously was sadly missing and a major improvement when it came to safer overtaking and extra power when it was needed.

But it was when driven as a semi-automatic that the revised city-coupé really excelled. Once again, the gear changes were smoother and quicker; in addition though, drivers now had the option of changing gear via a pair of steering wheel-mounted paddles, very much in a Formula 1 style. This proved to be a popular feature, and played a major role in transforming the whole city-coupé driving experience. For the first time ever, changing gear in a smart had become fun, fast, and very effective. smart's younger customers adored this significant improvement.

Almost as popular was the availability – at long last – of electric power-assisted steering on the

▷ **The jump in engine size from 599cc to 698cc provided later city-coupés with a useful boost to performance. Even the entry-level pure model now pushed out 50bhp. (smart UK)**

city-coupé, much appreciated by most potential buyers. Even in a car just 2.5m (8ft 2in) long, power steering was now seen as a 'must have'.

Handling-wise, the latest city-coupés were also a real improvement over their predecessors. Despite the early production smarts being generally considered safe and competent after the pre-production stability scares, smart was determined to improve things still further. That's why, by 2002, all new city-coupés came equipped with electronic stability program (ESP) – a feature originally developed for the forthcoming new roadster range, but which proved just as effective in transforming the city-coupé.

Replacing the previous TRUST PLUS driving control system (which itself had been very effective), ESP went a stage further. By making use

WHAT THE PRESS SAID: FORTWO

'A small car should ideally be just that – small. Easy to drive (especially for women), easy to park and at a cost the masses can afford (with at least a little help from car finance companies). In India, the closest you can get to such a car is the Maruti 800, or perhaps the Reva, which is a two-seater electric car. The answer can be found on the streets of Paris. The car, a diminutive two-seater, is a fashion icon in Europe and more than lives up to its name – the smart car.'

The Economic Times (India), March 2004

△ A 15 per cent increase in the city-coupé's torque levels meant a broader spread of power and a less frantic driving experience. The little smart was growing up fast. (smart UK)

of selective brake intervention to stabilise the car when needed, ESP also featured hill-start assist, brake assist, ABS and electronic brake-force distribution (EBD). It was the most technologically advanced package of handling enhancements ever seen in the city car class. This helped to give the highly developed new-generation city-coupé a head start in an increasingly competitive market.

There was also a rather welcome knock-on effect of ESP's excellence. It meant smart could soften the city-coupé's suspension settings, as well as introduce greater spring travel. It resulted in a vastly superior ride quality, something for which the original city-coupé had always been criticised. It made the latest models feel better developed, more grown up and far more comfortable – without losing any of their inherent fun appeal. It was a difficult balance to achieve, but smart did it admirably. Oh, and just in case these changes encouraged new owners to drive further in their smarts, the city-coupé now came with a larger fuel tank – which was handy.

NEW NAME, NEW ERA

A large number of relatively minor improvements and enhancements occurred during the early years of the city-coupé – full details of which appear at the end of this chapter. However, it was one of the city-coupé's most important single features that ended up being replaced completely

in 2003: its name. city-coupé had proved an effective badge for five years, but the start of a new era was just around the corner for smart, and the company decided that a new, more apt moniker was the order of the day.

These were exciting times for the company. The roadster and roadster-coupé models were being launched in 2003; the four-seater forfour was planned for 2004, and the formore SUV was due to take a bow in 2006. Somehow, the name city-coupé just didn't sit neatly amongst this fresh, modern line-up.

The chosen new name couldn't have been more logical. If a four-seater smart was going to be known as a forfour, the existing city-coupé could just as easily be re-branded as a fortwo. Obvious, wasn't it? That is exactly what happened and the fortwo coupé and fortwo cabrio arrived.

It was actually quite fitting that the city-coupé should finally have a new name; latest versions were, in so many ways, virtually new cars. In fact, the 2003 fortwo shared just 30 per cent of the components used in the 1998 city-coupé, according to smart. So the city-coupé faded away, replaced by the 70 per cent new fortwo – together with a simple new company logo that was to be used across the whole smart range. A new era had indeed begun.

The changes went down well with the motoring press of the time. Britain's *Auto Express* magazine, in January 2003, said: 'At last, the

▽ One of the most popular changes came when optional steering wheel-mounted paddles for the semi-auto gearchange were introduced. smart motoring had never been so much fun! (Author)

▽ Right-hand-drive cars were finally launched in October 2001, providing a useful boost to smart sales in the UK and opening up new opportunities in Australia and Japan. (smart UK)

△ Look closely and you'll see one of the most important changes to the city-coupé: its name was changed to fortwo, in keeping with the forthcoming new forfour. (Author)

smart feels like a "proper" car.' Their enthusiasm continued: 'With progress like this, the smart brand looks set to go from strength to strength.'

Quite incredible progress had been achieved in little more than four years. What had been potentially a corporate and financial disaster for smart had evolved into a strong product that people throughout Europe actually wanted to drive – and own. It was an amazing transformation.

FURTHER AFIELD

But why should the good folk of those original nine European markets be the only ones to enjoy the smart experience? Why indeed.

DaimlerChrysler never initially considered selling the smart city-coupé in the UK, as they considered British buyers too conservative to take to such a radical concept. What happened next though, showed the extent of consumer power. The smart was making headlines throughout the world, not least in the UK – and potential buyers began clamouring for the chance to buy a smart. A handful of unofficial importers and specialists began satisfying such demand, bringing over left-hand drive smarts and selling them at premium prices. Perhaps inevitably, this made DaimlerChrysler sit up and take notice.

The unofficial decision not to bring smart to

WHAT THE PRESS SAID: CITY-COUPÉ PASSION

'It might have won the hearts of a loyal band of owners, but the smart city coupé has always been something of a compromise. The combination of intelligent design, miracle packaging and limitless character has proven impressive, but performance, high-speed stability and transmission smoothness were left wanting. And although owners were willing to put up with these quirks, many potential buyers were put off. smart's engineers have listened to the criticism and taken action once again...'

Auto Express magazine (UK), January 2003

△ The new electronic stability program (ESP), originally developed for the forthcoming roadster range, helped transform the driver appeal of the city-coupé. It included brake assist, ABS and electronic brake-force distribution. (smart UK)

Britain was revoked and the first official imports went on sale through a couple of smart centres and via the Internet in January 2000. So good was the response that, by 2001, smart realised there would be an even bigger market if they tooled-up for right-hand drive production. This they did, and the first right-hook city-coupés went on sale in the UK in October 2001. The consumer had spoken and smart had listened.

This also meant other potential markets opening up for the city-coupé and, later on, the fortwo. With right-hand-drive smarts now in production, sales in other countries that drive on the left could be considered. Not surprisingly then, the steadily improving city-coupé was officially launched in Japan in November 2001 – the first time ever that a non-Japanese car with the tiny dimensions demanded by the tax-saving K-class light-vehicles sector had been sold there.

By 2002, smarts were also on sale in much of Eastern Europe, thanks to expansion into Hungary, the Czech Republic and the Slovak Republic. The same year saw exports to Taiwan get under way. Two years later, by the end of 2004, smart was making its presence felt in no less than 35 different countries.

But what about the world's biggest market – the United States? A tiny number of smart city-coupés found their way to the USA thanks to the determination of some eccentric enthusiasts – but, so far, that's been about it. The formore SUV of 2006 is the vehicle that will hopefully crack the American market for smart, but will the tiny fortwo ever officially be sold there? Only time will tell.

CRAZY CROSSBLADE

Like any manufacturer, smart has always been on the lookout for new ways to attract good publicity and generate great headlines. This was particularly important following the negative publicity of the early days. No wonder then, that by late 2000 – the second full year of city-coupé sales in Europe – smart had a rather impressive trick up

▷ **Right-hand drive smarts are now taken for granted. In the early years though, British enthusiasts had no choice but to take the left-hand-drive versions they were given. (smart UK)**

△ How mad was this? When smart showed off its new crossblade concept in 2001, enthusiasts hoped and prayed it would end up a production reality. (smart UK)

▽ It might look like the production crossblade at a glance, but the concept car had even more radical styling. Even so, things weren't toned down too much for the 'real thing'. (smart UK)

its corporate sleeve which was due to be revealed at the 71st Geneva Motor Show in February 2001.

It was known as the crossblade, an exciting concept car based around the smart cabrio. It took roofless motoring to a new extreme by also removing the cabrio's doors and windscreen, the latter being replaced by a narrow transparent wind deflector. Strength was maintained thanks to the TRIDION safety cell which was kept intact; attached though, were radically 'chiselled' body panels for a dramatic, futuristic new look.

The crossblade concept wouldn't have looked out of place in a moon-based sci-fi film. Its radical appearance was further enhanced by gloss-black body panels and TRIDION's titanium grey powder-coated finish. The combination looked mean, moody, and more than a bit mad!

Despite the crossblade concept's missing doors, the newcomer met all the latest safety standards of the time, aided by numerous high-strength bracing plates and a pair of robust aluminium side safety bars, to give TRIDION some useful back-up.

To say the crossblade idea created a storm at Geneva wouldn't be an exaggeration. It generated enthusiastic headlines throughout the world, prompting the most obvious question of all: would smart ever have the courage to put the crossblade into production?

Of course it would. Twelve months later, again at Geneva, the production-ready smart crossblade was unveiled, and it was announced that a full 2,000 examples would be produced in total. Fanatics who had enthused so much about the idea a year earlier could now get their hands on a crossblade.

This was the most exciting small car to be launched in a generation or more. The management at smart were confident of success, as Philipp Schiemer – marketing and sales director at the time – explained: 'The smart crossblade targets an exclusive clientele who attach great importance to personal freedom and independence. The open two-seater gives these customers a vehicle which expresses this outlook on life like no other product.'

Andreas Renschler, then chairman of the

▷ **And this is how the production crossblade finally looked, twelve months after the concept was unveiled. Potential customers were invited to form an orderly queue. (smart UK)**

◁ **With no doors, no windscreen and no roof, the crossblade was the maddest production car from any major manufacturer. Just 2,000 were to be made, announced smart. (smart UK)**

management board at smart, was particularly proud that the crossblade had made it to production reality in just twelve months: 'The fact that we have developed the smart crossblade within a year is further proof of the potential of our vehicle concept and at the same time it is a further step towards extending our product range.

'After the almost euphoric reactions at last year's Automobilsalon in Geneva, we have decided to offer this car to our customers.'

Indeed, but would the buyers come? The most famous customer of all was singer Robbie Williams, who took delivery of the first production crossblade in April 2002. He'd loved the crossblade concept from the moment he first saw it, and had

been in discussions with smart ever since to ensure he had the first of the 2,000 to be produced. Even so, he deliberately chose chassis number 0008 – for reasons best known to himself.

On delivery of his crossblade, Robbie enthused: 'Wow, I just love this car. It's innovative and unconventional, the two main qualities I look for in new projects.' The fact that he and smart had already been involved in some cross-publicity projects no doubt helped…

Just what was it that Robbie and all the other crossblade buyers loved about the newcomer? Probably that this was the nearest thing possible to a motorbike on four wheels. It was also a unique combination of fun and sensibility.

△ **Not the most sensible car for getting you to and from the golf club! No doubt smart's corporate tongue was very firmly in its cheek when this promotional shot was taken. (smart UK)**

▽ Who would buy the crazy crossblade? Well, Robbie Williams for one. He snapped up the first production example, although he insisted on chassis number 0008. (smart UK)

◪ A few crossblades – in left-hand-drive form only – did make it to the UK. Was there ever a more attention-grabbing car offered by any manufacturer? (smart UK)

The fun aspect was self-explanatory, particularly as the crossblade came with an electronically uprated 70bhp version of the city-coupé's three-cylinder engine. In any case, how could any car that looked this good and which was based on an updated smart cabrio not be fun to drive? As for sensibility … well, it was certainly safe; like all smarts, it came with full-size twin airbags, seat belt tensioners and belt-force limiters.

Even so, the crossblade wasn't a car anyone bought for sensible everyday transport. That wasn't even remotely the market it was aimed at. In fact, with no roof, no doors and no proper windscreen, its potential use was severely restricted in countries like the UK with its notoriously damp winters. But to criticise the crossblade for this would be to miss the point of its existence altogether.

Not everyone 'got' the crossblade, but it has been claimed that those who did soon found

themselves having more fun than the day they discovered sex. In an era when cars were being criticised for becoming too alike, this was a serious achievement on the part of smart.

CITY-COUPÉ CHANGES AND UPDATES

From its official launch in October 1998, the city-coupé was significantly altered and updated, even though some of the most worthwhile changes were hard to spot at first glance. So regular were the alterations that many enthusiasts now refer to them as different 'Mark' derivations of the city-coupé – obviously starting with the Mk1 to describe the earliest models. It should be noted though, that neither smart GmbH nor DaimlerChrysler has ever officially recognised the 'Mark' descriptions, even though members of the UK's thesmartclub use the terms freely.

Not all the changes in city-coupé specification were marked by any particular changes in chassis number format. However, one interesting point to look for on very early examples is whether the VIN number starts with 'TCC' or 'WME'. The former means the car was manufactured on or before 3 May 1999, when MCC was registered as a Swiss manufacturer; the latter means it was produced on or after 4 May 1999, by which time it was officially a German car company. It is only a minor point, but for aficionados of the original smart concept it's a crucial one.

Meanwhile, I am indebted to British smart fanatic Steve Smith for providing further information on the many and varied changes to the city-coupé's specification. Steve has been a member of thesmartclub for several years, as well as being a keen city-coupé owner.

▷ **Do you know your Mk1s from your Mk4s? The city-coupé's history is a complicated one, with early examples coming in for a whole raft of improvements and updates. It makes for fascinating reading though! (Author)**

△ The city-cabrio's 'peanut-style' headlamps proved so popular, they ended up being used across the city-coupé range from 2002. The first of these were unofficially known as the Mk6. (Author)

As we've already covered, what we now know as the Mk1 city-coupé was launched in left-hand-drive form in October 1998, coming in a choice of pure, pulse and passion models, as well as an early special edition known as the Limited/1. Officially the three main models were marketed as smart&pure, smart&pulse and smart&passion – although few owners now refer to them in this way. The entry-level pure was noted for its matt-black rear bumper and arches, as well as steel wheels and a solid plastic roof. As the cheapest model in the range, its standard power output was 45bhp.

Both the pulse and passion at that stage offered 54bhp versions of the same three-cylinder engine. The pulse came with 15-inch steel wheels fitted with centre caps, while the top-of-the-range passion boasted alloys.

When anybody refers to a Mk1 city-coupé now, they usually mean any example built from 1998 to early 1999, with the nominally altered Mk2 usually being of early to mid-1999 vintage. It was with the so-called Mk3 – introduced in the summer of 1999 – that more significant changes occurred, including the adoption of the TRUST-PLUS electronic traction and stability control system mentioned earlier. Another useful change was the adoption of a remote boot release button.

Late 2000 saw the Mk4 models arriving, which finally meant an end to the original-style washer jets that were mounted on the wiper arms; by moving the jets to a permanent fixing on the TRIDION safety cell, it allowed the use of standard looking wiper arms. Sadly though, the Mk4 city-coupé was the last model to use some of the extraordinarily vivid interior colours that had attracted so much attention on earlier examples; perhaps DaimlerChrysler felt it was time the city-coupé 'grew up' a bit? Worthwhile though, was a change to the car's front suspension, which saw the original leaf springs finally being replaced.

It was with the Mk4 city-coupé that official imports of left-hand-drive cars started arriving in the UK, although obviously there had been personal imports driving around since day one – and since the Mk1.

What many enthusiasts refer to as the Mk5 went on sale in 2001, complete with a newly updated and better quality interior – albeit finished mostly in grey. Meanwhile, passion models now came with colour-coded silver door mirrors instead of the previous black textured finish found on earlier top-of-the-range examples. Later the same year, right-hand-drive Mk5s went on sale in Britain, selling alongside left-hand-drive examples for a while until existing stocks of the latter were finally used up.

It was in 2002 that the cabrio's 'peanut-style' headlamps mentioned earlier in this chapter found themselves being used across the whole city-coupé range, making the Mk6 examples easier to spot at a glance. This coincided with the city-coupé's fuel tank being enlarged from 22 to 33 litres, making a huge difference to the car's non-stop cruising capabilities, as well as the fitment of a newly designed exhaust manifold and uprated turbocharger.

By March 2003, smart was launching what it officially called the 'second generation' city-coupé range – although most smart enthusiasts refer to this model as the Mk7. Confused? Perhaps that's not surprising. Even so, the Mk7 boasted some extremely useful updates, including use of the new, larger 698cc version of the previous three-cylinder engine. It also meant

the arrival of the much-praised ESP set-up, together with electronic brake-force distribution, improved traction control, hill-start assist and a greatly improved semi-automatic sequential-style transmission.

For the 2004 model year, the city-coupé was ready to receive its new name – becoming known as the fortwo range. However, these cars were identical to the Mk7 city-coupé in all but name and badge.

So … which 'Mark' city-coupé makes the best buy nowadays? Logically enough, most of the decision comes down to budget and individual requirements. At least now though, whichever 'Mark' you find yourself with, its identification should be that much easier; well, hopefully…

▶ **Officially referred to as the 'second-generation' city-coupé, most enthusiasts know this as the Mk7 – the last version before the complete change of name to fortwo. All Mk7s feature the larger, 698cc engine. (Author)**

SMART GETS SPORTY

With the success of the revolutionary city-coupé, it was only a matter of time before DaimlerChrysler began expanding the smart brand. It was a logical move; here was an all-new marque that was enjoying success throughout Europe with its debut model. Failure to exploit other sectors of the market would have been unthinkable – particularly for Mercedes, whose uncanny ability to spot new opportunities had been almost perfected by the end of the 1990s. It simply wasn't possible for smart to remain a single-model company if it was to survive long-term.

The dilemma for the smart management was which direction the marque should be taken in next. The two-seater city-coupé had created a whole new class of car upon its debut, effectively ensuring there were no direct rivals. Admittedly, it had to compete with similarly priced products, but none of them was even remotely similar in terms of specification or concept.

This time though, it would be different. Whichever model came next would have to compete with more obvious rivals, simply because there's a limit to how many brand-new sectors of the market can be created. It is little wonder then, that smart decided the next project had to be a sports car.

If you think about it, had smart's next move been to introduce a four-seater hatchback, critics would have accused the company of quickly losing its originality and foresight. Obviously, there is now a four-seater in the smart line-up, in the shape of the forfour; but it was important from a marketing angle and in terms of public perception that this arrived after the arguably more interesting sports car the designers had in mind.

HOW BIG, HOW EXPENSIVE?

The problem, of course, is that the sports car and convertible markets in both Europe and the USA are incredibly diverse. So where should a sporting smart be pitched in terms of size, price and specification? Not surprisingly, smart went for the lower end of the market; it needed a car that was smaller than the seriously ageing Mazda MX-5 and MG TF, with even more of the trendiness and funkiness that new-generation products like the Ford Streetka looked like providing.

However, in terms of inspiration for their newcomer, smart unashamedly took a step back in time to perfect their concept. In fact, by the time the smart roadster and roadster-coupé were

▷ **Which sector of the sports car market would smart compete in? The unveiling of the roadster concept gave a clear indication. Was this destined to be the MG Midget of the 21st century? (smart UK)**

▽ **With the TRIDION safety cell a major visual part of the roadster concept's chunky, sexy styling, this was instantly recognisable as a product of smart. (smart UK)**

▲ From the beginning, smart wanted its new sportster to offer a choice of two distinct styles. The roadster-coupé concept was an easy but very effective transformation. (smart UK)

ready for launch in 2003, smart was already making a feature of their nostalgic influences. They claimed the newcomer '…evokes memories of the compact and purist roadsters of the 1950s and 1960s. They reinterpret the purist roadster segment in form and design, coupled with today's demand for safety and comfort.'

It was easy to see where smart was coming from. You only have to look at how sports cars changed through the 1990s to realise how 'grown up' they suddenly were. Models like the MX-5 became bigger, heavier and less fun to drive. It was all a far cry from the halcyon days of the Sixties, when fun-loving young buyers could enjoy the charm and basic appeal of their MG Midgets, Austin-Healey Sprites and Triumph Spitfires. That end of the market had virtually disappeared.

Coming up with yet another Mazda MX-5 rival just wouldn't have worked for smart. Direct comparisons would inevitably be made, and smart would be desperately trying to break the stranglehold enjoyed by the world's best-selling

sports car. They could well have failed; and for any company owned by Mercedes-Benz, that simply wasn't acceptable.

Instead, a sporty smart had to have two vital ingredients. Most importantly, it had to be fun, not just fun in a wind-in-your-hair kind of way, but fun in terms of sharp steering, tight handling and an impressive power-to-weight ratio. It had to be a design of few excesses, yet instantly recognisable as a smart, even by those with little motoring knowledge.

It was a challenge, but by the time sneak photographs of concept smart roadsters started appearing in the world's press, it was obvious the stylists and designers were doing a fantastic job. And when visitors to Europe's various motor shows were first shown the smart roadster and roadster-coupé models in 2002, there was an air of genuine excitement. At last, it looked like one manufacturer had been brave enough to design a small, affordable and fun-to-drive sports car. A 'proper' sports car, if you like.

That the smart roadster and roadster-coupé didn't go on sale in mainland Europe until April 2003 was incredibly frustrating for thousands of potential buyers. But it was clever planning on the part of smart, who used the many months between the official unveiling and the actual on-sale date to keep interest and excitement high. It also brought added attention back to the smart brand throughout those months, which created a positive knock-on effect for the city-coupé.

The general consensus of opinion was that smart's designers and engineers had done well. In terms of making their newcomer instantly recognisable as a smart – even with all its badges removed – they couldn't have done any better.

Like the city-coupé before them, both the roadster and roadster-coupé made use of smart's now-famous TRIDION safety cell – a feature unique to the brand. This provided the newcomers with all the benefits of a modular construction, which in terms of build costs, ease of construction and any future restyles is a positive boon for DaimlerChrysler. Also, the added customer benefits of a lightweight bodyshell, ease of accident repairs and, of course, the unique two-tone appearance created by TRIDION couldn't be ignored.

Apart from its obvious functionality, as proved

▷ **Long before the official launch of the roadster range, the public was tantalised by images – like this – of how it would look. Rarely had a brand-new sports car been so eagerly awaited by enthusiasts. (smart UK)**

WHAT SMART SAID: A NEW APPROACH

'The market launch of the smart roadster and smart roadster-coupé is a first step towards extending the smart product range ... from a single product to multi-product brand. This change is reflected with a new company logo and new brand slogan: "Open your mind". The brand slogan applies to the customers, the products and the smart corporate philosophy. smart cars are innovative and offer their drivers individual solutions. smart drivers see the world with their eyes wide open; they are unprejudiced and open to new experiences.'

early on by the city-coupé's impressive performance in various crash tests, smart's TRIDION concept is without doubt the marque's most recognisable feature. It's almost inconceivable that a smart could ever be produced without making use of the TRIDION idea; for most enthusiasts, it just wouldn't be a smart.

It wasn't just TRIDION that gave the roadster and roadster-coupé their unique appearance however. For a start, these were small cars – a full 548mm shorter and 65mm narrower than the MX-5 of the time. They also featured incredibly short overhangs, large wheels and pronounced body-contoured wheelarches which, when combined with the roadster's low ride height, gave a uniquely sporty and sexy appearance.

Despite their diminutive dimensions, these new smarts featured an elongated bonnet and a two-seater passenger compartment set well back in the wheelbase. Both features led to a stance very much in the classic roadster style, which meant a fascinating amalgam of old and ultra-modern influences.

Both the smart roadster and roadster-coupé were instantly hailed as being like no other sports cars in their class, and in that sense, smart had achieved exactly what it set out to do in the first place.

BASIC SOPHISTICATION

Real achievement though, could only be claimed if smart's sporty new offerings were as fun to drive as their much-hyped pre-launch publicity had claimed. The downside of the public seeing a new model many months before they can actually go out and buy it, is that their expectations continue to rise throughout the long wait. If those first buyers of April 2003 weren't to be disappointed, the new roadster range had to be good to drive; damn good.

Happily, it was and still is. Despite fulfilling smart's original intention of being a basic sportster

WHAT SMART SAID: THE ROADSTER

'The dynamic, agile two-seaters from smart offer a unique driving experience where the focus is not on the destination, but on the journey there. The sporty, rear-wheel drive vehicles with the turbo engine familiar from the smart fortwo coupé and smart fortwo cabrio, but with more power and engine capacity, allow high lateral acceleration and therefore high cornering speeds.'

▽ The roadster and roadster-coupé shared the fortwo's 698cc three-cylinder turbocharged engine, albeit pumping out 80bhp here – which equates to an impressive 101bhp per tonne. (smart UK)

▽ In mainland Europe, a 61bhp roadster was available. It also went on sale in the UK for a short while, in left-hand-drive form only. (Author)

with a 1960s vibe, the newcomer was actually a very sophisticated piece of kit.

Not unexpectedly, power came from an uprated version of smart's eager little three-cylinder, six-valve turbocharged engine linked to the company's now-famous six-speed sequential semi-automatic transmission. The engine itself was slightly larger than that found in earlier city-coupés, although its 698cc capacity is now a feature of the renamed fortwo range. In roadster guise though, output is a distinctly healthy 80bhp at 5,250rpm, with 110Nm of torque at just 3,000rpm.

Well, 80bhp is what you get from most of the roadsters and roadster-coupés on sale. In many markets there's also a 61bhp derivative available, offering a cut-price route to sporty smart owner-ship. It has an obvious cost saving when new, as well as marginally cheaper insurance premiums – which can be crucial for young drivers. However,

it's the versions with '80 horses' that are (perhaps inevitably) proving the most popular.

At first glance, 80bhp from a two-seater sports car doesn't sound a great deal, and yet the opposite is the case. For a start, it's a truly impressive figure from just a 0.7-litre engine, and when it's fitted to a vehicle that weighs just 790kg, you suddenly end up with a rather useful power-to-weight ratio of 101bhp per tonne. Now that's more like it!

How did smart keep the weight so low? This was largely thanks to the TRIDION concept, which weighed in at a mere 192kg despite its incredible in-built strength and rigidity. It's the rigidity of TRIDION that also contributed to the roadster's impressive lack of scuttle shake, a major problem with some conventional sports cars. As with the city-coupé, the roadster also featured lightweight plastic body panels, which again kept weight down as well as easing any accident repair work.

▽ Starting off on a steep incline? No problem; smart's hill-start assist means less use of the handbrake and an easier drive. (smart UK)

▲ Looking for a sports car with plenty of equipment? The tiny roadster has the lot – including a handy cup holder in the back of the passenger seat! (smart UK)

Achieving the previously impossible dream of ultra light weight and exceptional strength and rigidity was just the start of the roadster's impressive features though. Even ignoring the tiny turbo powerplant and six-speed sequential transmission, the roadster's mechanical credentials shone through.

Described by smart as a 'driving dynamics control system', the roadster's ESP (electronic stability program) was similar to that now in use in the fortwo range. Its traction control set-up incorporated selective brake intervention, anti-stall assist, cornering brake control, electronic braking-force distribution and, of course, ABS. It was sophisticated by any standards; in what was basically a cheap and cheerful two-seater sports car, it was a phenomenal package.

To avoid being accused of taking all the excitement out of open-top motoring, smart included a facility for turning off the ESP system – via a simple push-button on the dashboard. This enabled the driver to create a certain amount of 'slip' of the rear wheels through rapid acceleration; however, for safety reasons, only the drive torque regulation and the selective brake intervention during the acceleration phase were actually deactivated. When braking, the selective brake intervention remained so as to stabilise the vehicle. It was a way of injecting a touch more character and fun into the car without making it in any way dangerous in the wrong hands, and it was a compromise that worked well.

Another useful feature was the roadster's HSA (hill-start assist) set-up, aimed at reducing the number of times a driver needed to use the handbrake during hill starts. After releasing the brake pedal, the wheels remained locked for 0.7 seconds – ample time for the driver to move his foot from the brake to the accelerator

WHAT THE PRESS SAID:
ROADSTER-COUPÉ

'Never have we driven a car that has attracted so much attention. The frog-eyed roadster coupé we took out became a real talking point, with most of the people we spoke to on our drive eager to find out more. True to smart tradition, the roadster-coupé is tiny; what's more, it's as well packaged as the ground-breaking city-coupé. With a surprisingly large boot at the front and plenty of storage under the glass hatch, it's reasonably practical, while a clever polystyrene and Velcro holder secures the glass panels in place if you wish to drive al fresco.'

Auto Express magazine (UK), September 2003

▷ **Even at a glance, the new roadster and roadster-coupé were smarts through and through. Shown here is one of the first UK-spec right-hand-drive coupés. (smart UK)**

◁ The sporty smarts' level of grip is astonishing, largely thanks to a sophisticated ESP system. Selective brake intervention, cornering brake control, ABS and anti-stall assist are all part of the package. (smart UK)

without the car rolling backwards or forwards. It was a genuinely useful feature which also helped prevent premature wear of the roadster's clutch.

As you would expect from any smart product, the new roadster line-up made some big claims when it came to safety – and not only because of that rigid TRIDION safety cell. Standard equipment included twin full-size airbags, seat belt tensioners and belt-force limiters, but it was the roadster's actual bodyshell design which provided the most protection.

Rear-end collisions were well catered for thanks to generously dimensioned side members in the boot floor and an extremely strong frame-type integral support that carried the whole drive unit and de Dion rear axle set-up. In addition, the 35-litre fuel tank between the passenger compartment and the rear axle was separated from the drive unit by a studded aluminium sheet and bulkhead.

Solid crossmembers helped reduce damage during side impacts, along with strong side skirts and B-pillars reinforced with high-strength sheet steel. The wide oval roll bar completed that little package. The doors, incidentally, were made of aluminium – an effective way of maintaining rigidity without adding excess weight.

The smart roadster and roadster-coupé certainly weren't lacking when it came to creature comforts and on-board goodies either. Standard equipment for the roadster in most markets included an electric soft-top, six-spoke 15-inch alloy wheels, electric windows, electric power steering, CD player and a leather-covered steering wheel and gear knob.

In addition, the roadster-coupé featured a two-piece removable hard-top, air conditioning and, of course, a glass fastback – which meant a tad more luggage space.

Which model looked the best? It's all down to personal preference, but you can't help admiring what smart achieved with one basic design. It's only at the rear that the roadster and roadster-coupé models differ in any significant way, although both cars look great from any angle. There's an argument that the roadster appears more 'raw', more sporting; yet somehow the roadster-coupé's proportions are so perfect, and so it's this version which many potential buyers end up choosing.

Me? I admire them both, but the practicality and overall balanced look of the roadster-coupé makes it my personal winner. Of course, you're allowed to disagree if you so wish…

Now then, it's no good having such a technically advanced mechanical and structural package at your disposal if the sports car you've just bought fails to excite you. After all, smart's main priority with the roadster and roadster-coupé was to create a fun experience at an affordable cost. The trouble with some hi-tech designs is that they

WHAT THE PRESS SAID: ROADSTER

'Getting the best out of the roadster is about building up momentum and hanging onto it, like in the old days when braking was for wimps. Luckily, the chassis is up to the job, and it surfs its way round corners chatting the whole time about exactly how much grip is left. It's just fast enough too, even if a 0–60mph time of 10.9 seconds isn't much to brag about. Crucially, it feels fast, mainly because it's like being strapped into a flying shoe. It's an enormously likeable little car. Huge fun, but in a healthy, low-cholesterol kind of way.'

Top Gear magazine (UK), April 2004

▽ fortwo drivers will recognise the steering wheel, the gearstick and most of the minor switchgear. Even so, the roadster's dashboard is very sporty looking. (smart UK)

▽ How smart-esque is that? The roadster's speedometer and tachometer are housed in two large pods straight ahead of the driver. (Author)

roadster-coupé, courtesy of smart UK. I didn't quite know what to expect; I'd driven plenty of city-coupés and fortwos in my time, but surely this was going to be a completely different experience? It was, and, despite my affection for and admiration of the fortwo, the difference with the roadster-coupé was definitely for the better. smart knew they had to create a dramatically different driving style to compete in the sports car scene; and that's exactly what they did.

The first thing you notice about both the roadster and roadster-coupé as you step in is just how low down you are. The seating position is incredibly low-slung, particularly when compared with models like the Mazda MX-5 and MG TF.

The second thing you notice is how smart's designers have carried over a lot of styling cues from the fortwo. The ignition key still slots in just behind the gearstick; the chunky steering wheel is essentially the same; the dashboard is very smartesque in style, particularly the two cowled pods ahead of the driver containing all the major instrumentation. The whole interior screams smart at you – and that's great news.

Anybody who has driven a fortwo will instinctively know how to pilot a roadster. The gearbox is identical, which means you have a choice between fully automatic mode or semi-automatic sequential changes – either via the stubby gearstick or through the steering wheel-mounted paddles. It's all very familiar stuff to existing fortwo owners.

What isn't familiar to many though, is the roadster's impressive turn of speed. On paper, these machines could easily be criticised for what looks like a lack of performance by sports car standards; a top speed of 109mph (175km/h) and a 0–60mph sprint time of 10.9 seconds (for the standard roadster) aren't spectacular in themselves. But there's far more to real fun motoring than figures alone. Where the roadster and roadster-coupé score is in their all-round driving experience.

Because you sit much lower than in any other similarly priced sportster, these roadsters feel drastically faster than their official figures might suggest. Get that 698cc three-cylinder motor working hard with the turbo spinning merrily, and you'll find yourself impressed by just how quickly

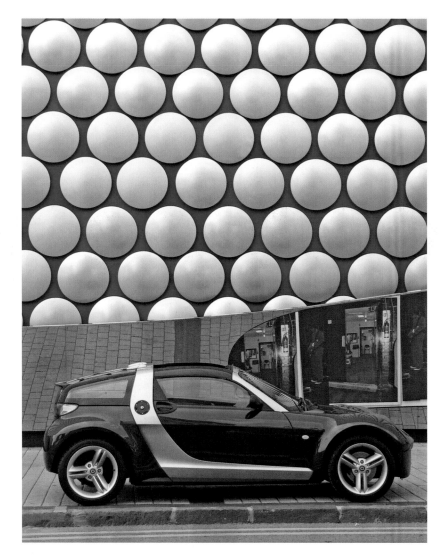

▲ **Now doesn't that look good? The stunning roadster-coupé parked up outside the equally impressive Selfridges store in Birmingham. (Author)**

become so anonymous and characterless, they lose most of their appeal.

smart customers needn't have worried. From day one, it became obvious the new roadster and roadster-coupé were out-and-out fun cars. Despite their prolific use of up-to-the-minute technology and electronic wizardry, they had the kind of fun factor that's sadly lacking from so many modern rag-tops. Those Midgets and Sprites of the early 1960s might have been basic in the extreme, but this new hi-tech roadster had managed to capture their essence and appeal – and had become the 21st century equivalent of those British classics.

This was proved to me the first time I drove a

Safety has always been important to smart, and the incredibly rigid TRIDION safety cell provides a huge amount of strength in the event of a crash. (Author)

The first roadster-coupé which the author drove – a press vehicle provided by smart UK – confirmed his suspicions: there's simply no other affordable sports car available that's this much fun to drive. (Author)

the sporting smart pulls away from the line. Making use of the paddles for the semi-auto gearchanges is by far the quickest method of gaining speed, as well as being the most fun. In fact, hard acceleration from standstill in any roadster makes life with a fortwo seem tame by comparison.

Despite this, driving a roadster at its limit is a drama-free experience. So effective is its electronic stability program, that it's incredibly difficult to upset the car's poise and agility. On those rare occasions when the rear end does prove a bit lively, it's easily brought back in line with some minor opposite lock, and all the while, the whole experience is putting the biggest grin on your face you'll have had in a long time.

The mid-range power of the roadster impresses even more, which means lots of fast, safe over-

△ Once you're aboard any roadster, you'll find plenty of room for a couple of six-footers. Gone is the cramped driving position associated with classic MG Midgets and Austin-Healey Sprites. (Author)

taking when the need – and the opportunity – arises. Keep that turbo working overtime and the revs high, and the roadster is a fast and nimble cross-country sprinter with grip and handling to match. Thanks to its mid-engined layout and its hi-tech suspension and braking systems, the roadster will actually outpace most bigger-engined 'rivals' when the roads get twisty, and for those enthusiasts who want to bring the fun back to modern motoring, that's a priceless feature.

After all, it's fun that these cars are all about. But that doesn't mean practicality has been forgotten altogether. Both the roadster and roadster-coupé offer a small but useful boot at the front, with a more usable amount of luggage space above the engine at the rear. The roadster-coupé's fastback design and large glass tailgate give it the edge over the standard roadster in

'open your mind', suggested smart in its new-for-2003 company slogan. The long-awaited roadster line-up was being heavily promoted throughout Europe. (Author)

terms of ultimate space, and if that's a big consideration for you, the coupé is the roadster of choice.

Whichever version you choose, you'll find the same surprisingly roomy cabin and fantastic driving position. Even those drivers well over six feet tall will find a position to suit, once they've manoeuvred themselves into place, while extra-tall passengers will be able to stretch out in comfort, so generous is the roadster's legroom.

The cabin itself, like the outside of the car, is finished to extremely high standards. The quality of the materials used throughout is superb, and the contemporary styling employed adds to the whole air of surprising sophistication.

Rarely – if ever – have I driven a compact sports car that's not only technically advanced but also enormous fun to drive. The two hardly ever go

together, but the smart roadster, is a sophisticated little funster that does its job brilliantly and with more character than just about anything else on the road.

Anybody who simply looks at the figures and assumes the smart roadster is outclassed as a performance sports car really does need to get behind the wheel. I challenge anyone to drive one for a few days and not fall in love with its charm, its fun appeal and its flamboyant character. I know I did.

WHAT'S AVAILABLE?

While in simple terms the sporting smarts are available in two versions – roadster and roadster-coupé – there are a few different variations on the same theme.

△ Buy a roadster or order a roadster-coupé with its optional fabric roof and this is what you'll get: an electrically operated soft-top that looks good open or closed. Removing the side roof bars (which are then stored under the front 'bonnet') makes the car feel even more like a 'proper' convertible. (Author)

Entry-level models in some markets are those 61bhp offerings mentioned earlier, with their poorer performance figures partially compensated for by obvious cost savings. These lower-powered models still feel surprisingly quick, mainly due to the roadster's ultra-low driving position and fantastic handling, enabling you to make the most of what performance there is. However, after a brief introduction to the UK market (in left-hand-drive form only), these models are no longer available to British customers.

So, as far as the UK is concerned, the cheapest of the lot is the roadster light, a stripped-out version that it is roughly 10 per cent less expensive than the simple-monikered roadster. It shares the same 80bhp engine as its more expensive cousin, but offers slightly improved

acceleration due to the weight saving. Inevitably though, it's not as popular as the rest of the range; most buyers of smarts, it seems, want some decent equipment levels as standard – and who can blame them?

Amongst the best-selling versions, the roadster comes next, followed by the roadster-coupé – which, in the UK, tends to be around £1,500 dearer. Is it worth the extra? It depends on whether you favour a removable hard-top over the pleasures of a 'proper' convertible; the latter arguably makes more sense for buyers concerned about security issues.

But what if you like the shape of the roadster-coupé, yet still hanker after a soft-top car? No problem. Amongst the roadster-coupé's lengthy list of optional extras is an electrically

operated soft-top to replace the rigid roof panels. When folded away, it sits neatly just behind the seats, and can be raised or lowered in only a few seconds at the flick of a switch. It's the ideal compromise when it comes to sports car thrills with a modicum of practicality.

At the top of the roadster pile, of course, sit the BRABUS roadster and BRABUS roadster-coupé. Well, it was inevitable, wasn't it?

THE BRABUS EFFECT

When those expert German modifiers going by the name of BRABUS decided to get in on the smart roadster action, it was obvious that something rather special would be the end result. The company has established an excellent reputation over the years for its heavily upgraded

Mercedes-Benz range, and the BRABUS city-coupé and fortwo models had already caused a stir throughout Europe. Enthusiasts couldn't wait to see what would happen when BRABUS got its enthusiastic hands on the roadster.

They weren't to be disappointed. The BRABUS roadster and roadster-coupé – now permanent members of the official smart line-up in almost every market – provided an exciting boost to performance, thanks to various modifications which included a new turbocharger, upgraded cooling system and a revamped engine management chip. The result was 101bhp from the high-revving 698cc three-pot – an increase of 19bhp over the standard model's 82bhp. Or, in other words, well over 20 per cent extra power.

That wasn't all, though. The BRABUS roadster and roadster-coupé – each priced in the UK within

▽ With some neat aluminium and leather detailing, the BRABUS roadster looked even more exclusive inside than the standard model. (smart UK)

◩ The roadster range got off to a flying start in every market it entered, surpassing all sales expectations in its debut year of 2003. Enthusiasts had waited a long time for its arrival. (smart UK)

£300 of each other at launch, the most expensive being a shade under £17,000 – also came with 17-inch alloys, a special BRABUS radiator grille, side skirts and body-coloured spoilers. The combination ensured a car with more 'attitude' and, some might say, a more masculine image.

Inside too, things had changed. Aluminium and leather detailing gave a more exclusive look to what was already a pretty funky design. Opinion is still divided as to whether the BRABUS internal changes were for the better, though.

Out on the road, other mods made themselves known. BRABUS had carried out upgrades to the standards roadster's suspension which, when combined with the enormous new tyres, gave an incredible amount of grip. Sadly though, not all of Europe's motoring press approved of these particular changes.

Nick Trott, writing for the UK's *Auto Express* magazine in March 2004, said: 'Quite simply, the huge new tyres offer far too much grip, and the low-geared steering means you're always winding on lock to get through tight bends. We can't help feeling that the original wheels and tyres, combined with standard suspension, would be more effective.'

This didn't stop Nick from liking the BRABUS roadster and roadster-coupé, though: 'Both smarts look fabulously chunky and expensive, plus provide masses of feel-good factor,' he reflected.

Even so, he made a good point about the BRABUS suspension and that wheel and tyre combination. If the standard roadster handles so brilliantly thanks to its highly developed chassis and its plethora of technological know-how, surely it could manage 101bhp without any need

for major changes? It would be fascinating to try a standard roadster with the BRABUS engine installed – and nothing else altered.

The launch of the BRABUS roadster range wasn't the first time those tuning experts had got their hands on the sportiest smart. In fact, in the roadster's production debut year of 2003, they initially came up with the completely outrageous roadster-coupé V6 bi-turbo – just ten of which were produced to show exactly how far the little smart could be developed.

The bi-turbo V6 boasted two of the standard model's three-cylinder engines joined together to create a 1,396cc twin-turbo V6. Power output was an astonishing 170bhp, with torque levels of up to 220Nm – both remarkable achievements from a 1.4-litre lump. In performance terms, this equated to a top speed of 137mph (220km/h),

▶ **Look familiar? The V6 bi-turbo's engine was actually made up of a pair of three-cylinder Suprex units from a standard roadster. A crazy idea that actually worked – brilliantly. (smart UK)**

It was only a matter of time before BRABUS got its hands on the sportiest smarts. The end result was more 'masculine' versions of both the roadster and roadster-coupé. (smart UK)

passing the all-important 62mph (100km/h) mark in only six seconds.

With so few bi-turbo V6 models created, smart enthusiasts assumed they'd never get the chance to see one 'in the flesh', but smart had other plans. After all, here was a fantastic marketing and promotional tool, guaranteed to hit the headlines wherever it went on show. So, during 2003, smart GmbH arranged for the BRABUS bi-turbo V6 to take part in various smart events throughout Europe – including Britain's London to Brighton smart rally, organised by thesmartclub. With around 1,500 smart owners from all over the UK taking part in the event, it was a great way of getting the bi-turbo V6 in front of as many enthusiasts as possible.

So what future plans do smart and BRABUS

have for the little roadster? Inevitably, there's plenty of frenzied activity going on behind the scenes, and I've no doubt that several other variations on a similar theme will be appearing in the years ahead. The roadster and roadster-coupé have far too much potential for it not to be exploited.

INSTANT SUCCESS

To say the smart roadster and roadster-coupé got off to a flying start would be an understatement. Orders had flooded in ever since the models were unveiled to the public in the autumn of 2002. By the time deliveries started in mainland Europe in April the following year, the sporty newcomers were almost guaranteed sales success.

Catch me if you can! Any BRABUS roadster will outperform many of its more expensive, bigger rivals. Crucially, it feels even faster than it is. (smart UK)

It's a mad, mad world! Never ones to rest on their laurels, BRABUS went a stage further with the roadster V6 bi-turbo – right up to 137mph (220km/h), in fact. (smart UK)

During the remaining eight months of 2003, smart GmbH claimed they would be happy if the roadster and roadster-coupé managed to sell 8,000 units between them. By the time the year drew to a close, though, no fewer than 20,200 examples had been built. And, amazingly, the roadster and roadster-coupé had already established themselves as the second best-selling sports cars in their class in countries like Germany, France and Switzerland.

Right-hand-drive examples of the roadster and roadster-coupé went on sale in the UK in September 2003, following official imports of a limited number of left-hand-drive, 61bhp examples earlier in the year. And as Europe's biggest market for convertibles, it was essential for smart that the roadster succeeded.

Watch it go! Despite just a 1.4-litre powerplant, the V6 bi-turbo would hit 60mph (97km/h) in a mere six seconds. Sadly, only ten examples of this amazing machine were to be built. (smart UK)

Success did, of course, follow. As did major disappointment, for on 1 April 2005 smart GmbH announced that, as part of a new business plan for the company, production of both the roadster and roadster-coupé would cease by the end of the year. DaimlerChrysler was desperate to reduce operating losses at smart – and, despite healthy sales levels of the two sportsters, neither model had ever made a profit. The cars that had brought sporting motoring to a whole new generation of enthusiasts would be no more.

It was a bitter blow to fans of the roadster and roadster-coupé, but there was no going back. After several years of stressing the need to expand the range of smart models on offer, DaimlerChrysler was backtracking like never before. The roadster and roadster-coupé weren't earning their keep in profitability terms, and so they had to go.

After just three years of life, it was a sad and premature end for two of the most interesting, most fun-to-drive sports cars of the 21st century. Both the roadster and roadster-coupé would be sadly missed.

▷ Not everyone was overwhelmed by the BRABUS roadster's capabilities; motoring journalist Nick Trott criticised its wheel and tyre combination. (smart UK)

A FAMILY AFFAIR

While the previous chapter details the reasons why smart decided to launch a sports car as its second product line, the company knew it couldn't ignore more mainstream sectors of the market forever. And neither did it intend to; if smart was going to increase annual productivity to the level where it was profitable in the long-term, it was essential that there was a model which could compete within a far larger sector of the market.

The most logical sector for smart to tackle next was that of the 'supermini'. It already had the city car segment sewn up with the city-coupé, shortly to be renamed the fortwo, so moving up to the next class was a logical step. But what exactly would smart's main rivals be?

The 'supermini' market is a complicated one. It starts off at a very affordable level, with the most basic versions of the Fiat Punto, Vauxhall/Opel Corsa, Nissan Micra, Citroën C2, Renault Clio and the like, all available in most European markets with temptingly low starting prices. They're a size up from the city car class, and yet their keen pricing means they're still fantastic value in basic trim. But these were exactly the kind of hatchbacks smart did not want to try competing with.

Under DaimlerChrysler ownership and with massive improvements to its products since those mad, bad early days, smart was determined to pitch itself as a premium brand in whichever new market segment it entered. So, trying to offer a four-seater family-sized smart for the same price as an ultra basic Punto or Corsa just wasn't on the agenda. No, smart was looking a little further upmarket than that.

In fact, smart was looking fairly and squarely in the direction of BMW's MINI. Here was a retro-styled three-door hatchback that managed to combine premium pricing with a trendy image, top build quality and the kind of residuals that left rivals trailing in its wake. It represented exactly what smart hoped to achieve – although any smart product would inevitably need to swap retro appeal for a more contemporary look.

The MINI was not the only 'supermini' smart had its corporate sights set on. It realised buyers were also willing to spend not inconsiderable sums of money on top-of-the-range Volkswagen Polos – another car with a perceived high quality, for which buyers were happy to pay a premium. The Polo might not have looked exciting, but customers saw it as a safe bet, a quality product and one that was worth paying a bit extra for.

▷ **Have you met my big brother? smart desperately needed a larger model than its ever-popular fortwo if it was to achieve the extra sales that could lead to profitability. (smart UK)**

▽ **Sales of the VW New Beetle may have been on the decline in many European markets, but the MINI could do no wrong. To compete with both, smart needed a design-led product to capture buyers' imaginations. (smart UK)**

◁ Preliminary sketches officially released by smart showed how the production forfour could look when launched in 2004 – albeit a more rakish version! (smart UK)

smart understandably wanted a piece of this particular action.

What it wanted to avoid though, was going down the same road as Volkswagen's New Beetle. Although larger than a 'supermini', it was – like the MINI – a retro-styled, head-turning product that had got off to a strong start in most markets. However, its novelty had begun wearing thin after a few years on sale. It found itself criticised for being the automotive equivalent of 'all fur coat and no knickers' – in other words, a car that looked cool for a while and attracted plenty of attention, but whose deeper appeal or technological advances were sadly lacking. smart had to make sure their new family car was a much longer-lasting attraction.

OUTSIDE HELP

Work began on designing the new family smart – but exactly in which direction should it go?

In terms of concept, there was really only one option: the newcomer had to use the existing and instantly recognisable TRIDION safety cell idea if it was to be a 'proper' smart. It was such an important part of the company's brand values and identity that to have a non-TRIDION smart in the line-up would have been unthinkable.

Even so, that didn't mean much of the rest of the car couldn't be conventional in its layout. With that being the case, it opened up all kinds of possibilities in terms of collaboration with other manufacturers.

Co-operation and collaboration are two of the buzzwords in today's global motor industry. They help to reduce development costs for brand-new models, without going to the extent of creating mergers and takeovers along the way. By the time thought was being given to the idea of a four-seater smart at the turn of the Millennium, even a company the size of DaimlerChrysler wasn't beyond benefiting from cross-development with other manufacturers.

DaimlerChrysler already had a sizeable ownership stake in Mitsubishi, but which, in percentage terms, was actually reduced by the summer of 2004 … though that's another story. The relationship had worked well; in certain key markets, for example, the Mitsubishi Canter commercial vehicle was distributed and marketed by DaimlerChrysler, but it was an open secret that a more in-depth working relationship – based around future car designs – was in the pipeline.

That's why what we now know as the smart forfour was developed in co-operation with Mitsubishi, and that's why the new-for-2004 Mitsubishi Colt shared many of its underpinnings with the smart. It saved both companies a not-so-

▷ **Beneath the skin, 60 per cent of the forfour was the same as the new Mitsubishi Colt. All petrol engines in the range were courtesy of the Japanese company. (smart UK)**

small fortune in development costs, and it enabled them to share production facilities at Mitsubishi's Dutch plant. It was a relationship that benefited both companies, but perhaps it's DaimlerChrysler's smart brand that shone through as the real winner.

A PROPER SMART?

Although most potential buyers probably couldn't care less where their cars are built, some smart enthusiasts weren't so convinced when the forfour was officially unveiled at the Geneva Motor Show in early 2004. For a start, it was produced at a factory in Holland more used to building Mitsubishis – which meant its relationship with the smartville plant at Hambach was non-existent. Then there was the car itself…

Here we had a front-engined, front-wheel-drive, normally aspirated, five-door family hatchback. Proper smarts, argued enthusiasts, had engines at the back; they were rear-wheel drive; they used idiosyncratic powerplants and turbochargers, and they were among the most entertaining cars on the road – at any price. Could a new smart 'supermini' with such traditional underpinnings ever be considered a real smart?

It was a fair point. smart fanatics loved the offbeat layout and characterful engine note of their city-coupés, fortwos and roadsters. Would they really take to a newcomer that – beneath its plastic skin – was little more than a Mitsubishi Colt? Perhaps, but smart GmbH wasn't just aiming the new forfour at existing smart owners looking for an upgrade; they also had to aim the newcomer at the kind of folk who were buying MINIs if it was to stand any chance of serious commercial success. And for the average buyer of

▽ **Many options were put forward by DaimlerChrysler's designers before the final look of the forfour was decided upon. Creating a mainstream car that's both individualistic and contemporary was no mean feat. (smart UK)**

△ With front-wheel drive, a front-mounted engine and a conventional transmission as standard equipment, the forfour was the least idiosyncratic of all smarts upon its launch. (smart UK)

own; when they're done properly they can work wonders.

This was one of the best examples of a healthy working relationship. Mitsubishi had a new Colt that was very much a Mitsubishi, albeit developed primarily with the European market in mind, while smart ended up with the forfour, which was instantly recognisable as a smart. The two individual brand identities, despite being so disparate, had remained intact throughout the whole project, and in that sense, the new forfour was surely a triumph.

THE SAME ONLY DIFFERENT

△ In the 'supermini' class, this is what most purchases get used for – the all-important weekly shopping trip! With black panels to match the black TRIDION, this particular forfour looks impressively different. (smart UK)

an upmarket 'supermini', rear-mounted engines and sequential-style gearchanges weren't high on the list of priorities.

But while the forfour's mechanical layout was similar to almost all its direct rivals, smart followers could take comfort from knowing that everything else about this family hatch was different. In fact, put a forfour and a 2004-model Mitsubishi Colt alongside each other and you'd be hard pressed to spot any real relationship between the two. This is where all the advantages of clever platform sharing, joint development and cross-company production facilities really come into their

Despite sharing 60 per cent of the components that you can't see with its Mitsubishi Colt cousin, the smart forfour is a very individual-looking machine. It's instantly recognisable as a smart whichever angle you're viewing it from for the first time, and in an age of look-alike family cars, this has to be a huge marketing advantage.

Whether you consider the forfour to be something of a looker … well, that's obviously a subjective matter. Personally, I think smart's stylists have done a superb job, despite – or maybe because of – what had to be the forfour's deliberately controversial aesthetics. By today's

⚠ **The front and rear light treatment of the forfour helps to really set this five-door hatchback apart from its major rivals. (smart UK)**

standards, for example, the window area looks incredibly shallow (either that or the waistline looks almost bizarrely high), and yet, rather than giving the vehicle as a whole a dated stance, it looks more modern than just about anything else in its class.

That is aided, of course, by the forfour's use of the tried and trusted TRIDION safety cell and plastic body panels approach. Like the rest of the smart line-up, this results in a two-tone appearance which helps to break up the forfour's styling, providing it with a less 'heavy' look. It also gives it less weight in reality too, as the whole car comes in at well under one tonne – an impressive achievement for a five-door hatchback with great claims being made about its safety and strength.

It's not just TRIDION that gives the forfour its unique appearance. Wander round a forfour, take in all the details and you'll see what I mean. The quad ovoid headlamps set into the front panel; the broad-grinned front grille; the twin air intakes in the bonnet; the steeply sloped windscreen set well forward; the dramatic rear lights that effectively replace any traditional C-pillar, and the seriously flared wheelarches which help to give the whole design a more squat and sporty look. All these styling features combine to make the forfour one of the most individualistic five-door

hatchbacks currently on sale anywhere in the world.

All of which was achieved without employing any of the 'retro cuteness' that designers of the MINI and the New Beetle had to resort to in order to attract style-conscious buyers with high disposable incomes. The new forfour looked like it could achieve all this – and more – by being cool, contemporary and more than a bit classy.

While the idea of a TRIDION safety cell clad with plastic body panels obviously wasn't new for smart, it was revolutionary stuff within this particular market sector. Beneath that skin though, things were deliberately much more conventional. They had to be – partly because of the restrictions dictated by the joint development with Mitsubishi, and also because the forfour's buyers were likely to be slightly less radical in their thinking than fortwo owners.

Even so, smart fanatics were delighted to discover that at least one three-cylinder engine was on offer – the entry-level 1,124cc six-valve three-pot developed by Mitsubishi. Despite not offering the same 'Engineered by Mercedes' boast of the fortwo and roadster engines, this particular three-cylinder lump was similar in character, being eager, high revving, great sounding and damn good fun when pushed hard. Its 74bhp output

might not have been class-leading amongst other premium 'superminis', but when combined with the forfour's lightweight design it felt quite quick – certainly far livelier than its maximum speed of 102mph (164km/h) and its 0–62mph (100km/h) sprint time of 13.4 seconds might suggest.

More mainstream in appeal than that smallest engine were, of course, the forfour's 1,332cc and 1,449cc four-cylinder eight-valve units, developing 95bhp and 107bhp respectively – both excellent figures for engines of this size. For the 1.3, it meant a top speed of 111mph (179km/h), with the 1.5 managing 118mph (190km/h) flat out. Nought to 62mph (100km/h) acceleration times came in at 10.8 and 9.8 seconds respectively – again, perfectly respectable within this class.

Like the three-cylinder unit, the two four-cylinder petrol engines had been developed by Mitsubishi and were soon being praised by the motoring press for their gutsy feel and get-up-and-go character. They weren't necessarily the

◁ Apart from the TRIDION influence of the design, it's the forfour's styling details that help to give it its unique appearance: the four ovoid headlamps; the wide-mouthed front grille and the enormous rear lights that dominate the C-pillar. It's a fascinating mix. (smart UK)

◁ The performance
figures of the 1.5-litre
forfour may not have
looked spectacular, but
this fun-to-drive
hatchback felt lively –
very much like a
'proper' smart.
(smart UK)

most refined powerplants within the 'premium supermini' class, but that didn't necessarily mean problems ahead. After all, the MINI's engine was rarely praised for being the best around, but this had had absolutely no effect on sales of the car; far from it, in fact. At least any engine developed by Mitsubishi for use in a smart would surely be reliable?

Even so, there were some smart buyers who insisted on Mercedes engineering to power them along – which meant they had to look towards the forfour's diesel range which went on sale in most of Europe in August 2004. This comprised a 1.5-litre three-cylinder turbo-diesel design, with outputs of 68bhp or 95bhp depending on the version buyers chose. Aside from their enviable claim that they had been designed and developed by Mercedes, these diesel-powered models were vital to the future success of the forfour.

While sales of diesel-engined cars in the 'city' sector of the market have traditionally been in the minority, no new 'supermini' can hope to achieve serious sales success without at least one diesel engine in its line-up. No longer are diesels seen as dirty, noisy and completely lacking in driver appeal; now there were some distinctly sporty

small diesel cars on sale (SEAT Ibiza Tdi 130 Sport and Skoda Fabia 130 vRS amongst them), and smart needed to tap into this market if it was going to make an impression on the sales charts.

Whichever engine – petrol or diesel – that forfour buyers chose though, they had a very smart-like choice when it came to transmissions. More traditional 'supermini' drivers could opt for the forfour's standard five-speed manual set-up, the same as that found in the Mitsubishi Colt, and a fine job it did too, thanks to its fairly slick feel. But the more smart-minded customers, who had always admired the company's six-speed semi-automatic sequential set-up from the fortwo and roadster ranges, could specify this in the forfour.

Uprated and improved, the sequential change was faster and more effective in the forfour than it felt in even the later fortwo models. Even so, it seemed to be at its best when linked to the forfour's entry-level three-cylinder 1.1-litre engine. Maybe it was because of that particular unit's rev-happy nature and its fun-sounding engine note; or perhaps it was because it made the cheapest forfour feel the most like a grown-up fortwo. Either way, a keenly priced forfour 1.1 ordered with the sequential-style gearbox was a great way of taking the boredom out of family-style motoring.

WHAT THE PRESS SAID: FORFOUR

'The revvy powerplants make their presence felt at all times, but even the smaller-capacity petrol units are gutsy and pull from low speeds, especially the three-cylinder 1.1 with its mad, warbling engine note. Although the manual gearbox has well spaced ratios and a short, snappy shift, the automated six-speed is a better bet. While it still features a slightly ponderous upchange, it is a vast improvement on the automated gearboxes in other smart models. It is also super-fast on the way down the ratios and, while the steering wheel-mounted paddles are not well sited, they are easy to use once you get accustomed to them.'

Auto Express magazine (UK),
February 2004

INSIDE INFORMATION

The interior of the forfour created almost as many headlines for the newcomer as did its external styling when it was seen officially for the first time in early 2004. Here was an interior that showed imagination, creativity and an abundance of style – three facets sadly lacking in so many of the forfour's obvious rivals.

The biggest internal feature of the forfour was what smart referred to as 'the ingenious new lounge concept' – which basically enabled plenty of variations of use inside the car. The back rests of the two front seats, for example, could be folded down so they were almost level with the rear seats to create a large horizontal seat surface – ideal for 'chilling out' or when parked up for a rest. The rear seat bench could also be adjusted by 150mm in length, while rotatable arm rests made sure you could always find a relaxing position.

 So this is what they meant by the 'lounge concept'. The forfour boasted the kind of thoughtful interior touches you'd normally associate with an MPV. (smart UK)

that didn't rely on nostalgia or retro appeal to get itself noticed.

A HEAD START

But was success guaranteed for the new forfour? Early signs certainly looked promising and even before the official unveiling of the new four-seater, more than 150,000 potential buyers in Germany had expressed an interest in the car. Hopes were high that smart had another success story on their hands – and, this time, one that wouldn't take several years to get itself established.

The obvious advantage the forfour had in terms of immediate appeal was the strength of the smart branding by the time it went on sale in 2004. This was unlike in 1998, when the city-coupé wasn't just a new model but a whole new marque. Six years later, the smart brand was known and respected in 31 countries throughout

▷ As soon as you climbed aboard any forfour, you instantly knew you were in a smart. The interior styling and detailing screamed brand values to driver and passengers alike. (smart UK)

Then there was the forfour's abundance of handy cup holders and storage compartments – more akin to a cleverly designed MPV than a MINI-rivalling hatchback. This was a fantastically well thought out interior by any standards.

In keeping with the blatant hint given by its name, the forfour was always intended as a four-seater and nothing more. The standard rear seat layout, with its heavily sculpted shaping, made sure of this. However, those buyers who demanded an occasional five-seater for their money could pay extra for a reshaped rear bench seat, together with an extra head restraint and additional three-point seat belt. The choice was there, but with the target buyer being the young professional, the standard four-seater layout looked like being the most popular.

Whatever the layout, each forfour interior was a bright, colourful and airy place to be. This applied to the dashboard layout as much as it did the choice of four different hues and two different trim levels – pulse and passion. The dashboard and fascia were typically smart in style, with two main instrument pods straight ahead and with the whole design looking cool, contemporary and aspirational. Once again, smart had managed to come up with a trend-setting, desirable design

WHAT THE PRESS SAID: FORFOUR

'The forfour is actually the fruit of co-operation between smart (owned by Mercedes) and Mitsubishi. Most of what you can't see is shared between this car and the upcoming Mitsubishi Colt. The basics were designed by Mitsubishi, while Mercedes contributed the diesel engines, the semi-automatic transmission and the electronics.'

The Independent (UK), March 2004

◁ Normally a four-seater (hence the name), the forfour can be specified with an optional three-person back seat if buyers so wish. (smart UK)

the world; and by the end of 2004, the number would be increased to 35, including the potentially important Canadian market. The forfour was a brand-new model from a well-respected name – and that alone would give it a vital head start over its rivals.

Like the other smart models, the forfour had a number of 'unique selling points' in its favour. Plastic body panels that could resist minor knocks and scrapes, for example, gave the forfour an obvious (and typically smart-like) advantage in the urban market, and the kind of looks that guaranteed double takes and smiles of admiration from passers-by giving the forfour obvious appeal to the most attention-seeking of buyers. But even in boringly practical terms, the latest from smart seemed to make a lot of sense.

For a start, here was a car that was usefully larger than its MINI arch rival – a full 126mm longer, in fact. In a market where the novelty of trendiness and fashion can start to wane after a while, this was an important advantage. It meant the smart was roomier than the MINI – and that was a vital plus point against a car that had been criticised for its lack of space and its cramped nature. It meant the smart could win friends not just because of its looks but through its ease of ownership, too.

◁ German interest in the forfour was particularly high prior to the model's launch. But could yet another five-door 'supermini' really shake up the market and achieve sales success? (smart UK)

AND TO FOLLOW?

Even before the forfour hit the streets, smart was making no secret of the fact that a new, fourth model range was in the pipeline. And this time it was a model destined to go on sale in the USA, a country that had so far managed to steer clear of the smart master plan – despite being the world's largest car market.

The delay in getting smart into the USA was understandable; it had to be timed to coincide with the launch of a vehicle that would actually suit American tastes. No wonder, therefore, that smart's next move was to announce the development of an all-wheel-drive SUV – which in most dictionaries stands for Sport Utility Vehicle, but in smartspeak means smart utility vehicle. It was logical. America buys more 4x4s than any other country; they simply can't get enough of

them. So smart was understandably keen to grab a slice of that particular action.

What smart told us about its new formore model was that it would be a relatively compact 4x4, and the company even released preliminary sketches to give us a hint of how it would look. From first impressions it promised to be a good-looking, ultra-cool, compact 4x4 quite unlike anything else available in its class.

The formore was to be unique within the smart range too, for being built at DaimlerChrysler's Brazilian factory in Juiz de Fora. By the time the formore was to arrive in 2006, smart's four-model line-up would be the products of three different plants in three different countries. Throw into the equation the large engine plant in Germany and you had a four-country mix, making this one of the most 'cosmopolitan' of all modern car brands. That certainly fitted in well with the smart ethos, even though many enthusiasts would always see the smartville plant in France as the natural home of car.

The dawning of 1st April 2005, however, saw a major change of direction for smart, with the announcement by DaimlerChrysler of a new business plan for the company and an almost complete reversal of previous intentions. Now, not only were the highly praised smart roadster and roadster-coupé models to be discontinued by the end of 2005 (as detailed in the previous chapter), but the forthcoming smart formore was being cancelled altogether. Quite simply, there was to be no smart 4x4.

It was a bitter blow to the engineers who had been working on the project, as well as to smart fans worldwide who were looking forward to a fourth model line. Now, it seemed, the smart line-up would be back to just two individual ranges: fortwo and forfour. Although smart itself had been saved, half of its eventual four-model line-up had become casualties of major rationalisation.

So what went wrong exactly? DaimlerChrysler, fed up with smart failing to make any profit, saw a need for drastic action if it was to achieve its new goal of break-even for smart by 2007. The forfour would continue in production with the co-

▽ **The smart formore 4x4 was originally scheduled for launch throughout Europe and the USA in 2006, meaning a fourth model line-up for the brand. By April 2005, though, plans had changed and DaimlerChrysler announced the scrapping of the entire formore project. (smart UK)**

By 2004, smart's product range looked bigger and healthier than ever, a far cry from the uncertain days of 1998 and the city-coupé's launch. Rationalisation in 2005, however, saw the roadster and roadster-coupé models discontinued by the end of the year. (smart UK)

operation of Mitsubishi and, thanks to what DaimlerChrysler called '…measures to improve profitability', would hopefully break even in the future. The main emphasis, though, would be on intensified development of the fortwo's successor and that model's launch into the American market.

With competition in the city car sector increasing throughout the life of the fortwo, an all-new replacement was exactly what smart reckoned was needed to guarantee future success – and even survival. That's why all efforts were suddenly being steered towards a successor at the earliest possible opportunity. But this in itself brought major challenges for smart's engineers, not least the work needed to make the 'new fortwo' suitable for sale in the USA.

The existing fortwo model had been shown at the 2005 Detroit Motor Show and received an impressively positive reaction. Research by smart suggested a market for its replacement in the USA did exist, hence the sudden urgency to put this plan into action. It might not have been the smart that American buyers originally thought they were getting, but the new-generation fortwo was apparently what appealed to them the most. Or so smart hoped.

With American sales set for the future, the fortwo's economies of scale could be dramatically improved, aided by a plan to sell its next-generation three-cylinder petrol engine to other car companies where possible. It all seemed to make financial sense, and that's what mattered to the DaimlerChrysler board – and to everybody concerned about the future survival of smart.

Even so, for smart enthusiasts everywhere it was a truly sad day when news of the company's rationalisation programme hit the headlines.

IT'S A PEOPLE THING

The smart brand holds a unique position in today's new-car market for its aspirational appeal to real fanatics. Nobody buys a new or second-hand smart because they simply want sensible transport; invariably they're also attracted by the funky styling, the overdose of charisma and the sheer fun appeal. This is particularly true when it comes to the fortwo and roadster ranges, two of the most characterful and individual car designs available anywhere, at any price.

Perhaps the only other affordable new car to attract a similarly high proportion of genuine enthusiasts amongst its buyers is the MINI. But that, of course, is essentially a single-model marque. smart, on the other hand, manages to attract the same percentage of car-fanatic buyers across its entire line-up. And it's this that puts the brand in the enviable position it is in today.

It wasn't always that way. As explained earlier, there were so many problems surrounding the early years of the smart city-coupé project that the prospect of it ever becoming an enthusiasts' cult car seemed remote in the extreme. But, happily, those troubles were overcome and the city-coupé found itself becoming the darling of the urban car world.

THE AFFORDABLE ICON

The word 'icon' is one that's seriously abused by the world's car manufacturers and even the motoring press. Very few new vehicles on sale today can genuinely be proclaimed as icons, and those that can be are so often out of the financial grasp of many buyers. The smart city-coupé and fortwo – and, increasingly, the roadster and roadster-coupé – are different however. These much-loved machines are now held in such high esteem and have broken so many design thresholds, that to describe them as icons of 21st century life wouldn't be an exaggeration.

So just who is it that's put these cars in such an extraordinary position? Who actually buys them, loves them, cherishes them and spends serious money uprating them? The simple answer is: anyone, and everyone.

Contrary to what Swatch and Mercedes-Benz might have predicted way back in the mid-Nineties when development of the smart concept was well under way, there is no typical buyer out there to personify the brand. Purchasers are surprisingly evenly split between men and women

▷ **The annual London to Brighton smart run attracts large numbers of fanatics from all around the UK and Europe. This rare crossblade was among those taking part in 2002. (smart UK)**

▽ **No new car brand can boast such fanatical owners as smart; it's a way of life! This modified city-cabrio with appropriate registration number certainly turns heads. (Author)**

△ An impressive proportion of smart city-coupés and for-twos are now owned by companies looking for cost-effective, chic urban transport and an unbeatable promotional tool. (Author)

▽ A city-coupé makes a great camera stand when you're out and about! Just one of the many different uses that owners have invented over the years... (Author)

(unlike most other city cars, bought predominantly by women). Also, despite the city-coupé being designed primarily as a city-based commuter car, there are just as many buyers from the suburbs and semi-rural areas as there are from the biggest European cities.

It's a similar story when it comes to the age of the average smart buyer – if such a thing as an 'average smart buyer' actually exists, of course. During research for this book, I've met up with countless smart owners, and what is obvious is that there's no natural demographic for the marque. Owners I've encountered have ranged from 17 years of age to some well into their seventies, and it's a similar story throughout Europe and beyond. Despite producing youthful, trendy, design-led products, smarts are bought by every major adult age group.

Impressive numbers of smarts are also bought through businesses, with thousands of companies around the globe realising the promotional benefits of a sign-written smart outside their premises. This is particularly the case in cities, where shops, restaurants and nightclubs have made the most of the city-coupé's and fortwo's head-turning looks to publicise their own companies. smarts have even been bought as urban delivery vehicles, offering the manoeuvrability, low running costs and reliability demanded by courier drivers; they get the job done and they attract positive publicity in the process.

CLUBBING TOGETHER

For evidence of just how much the world has taken to smart, you need look no further than the scores of thriving smart clubs – particularly throughout Europe. Take a look at where smart's sales are healthiest and you'll find at least one – but usually several – clubs dedicated to the marque and its owners.

This is an almost unprecedented situation for any new make or model. Car clubs tend to be associated more with the classic car scene, and yet the best smart clubs are attracting a near fanatical following.

Unlike the world of classic cars, it seems, the vast majority of smart owners tend to be computer savvy and regular users of the Internet. That's why most smart clubs are Internet based, with members keeping in touch with each other via message boards and forums, with newsletters and information sheets also usually available online. It's a fantastic way of contacting fellow smart owners throughout the world – and it can get quite addictive.

▷ Any idea what the collective noun is for a gathering of smart owners? The smart social scene is one of the most active and best supported you'll find anywhere. (Author)

How's this for a great pairing? At a glance, Al Young's registration numbers read WEE CAR and WEE TOY. Neat! (Al Young, Chairman, thesmartclub)

The biggest of the smart clubs, it is claimed, is Britain's logically named thesmartclub, full details of which can be found at www.thesmartclub.co.uk. The club's official line is that it is 'The world's largest independent club for DaimlerChrysler smart car owners and enthusiasts' – which means there are several thousand people signed up for free membership – and who can blame them? Membership benefits include access to the member areas of the website, a discount card for various smart specialists, technical advice via online fact sheets, an annual track day event and convoy to the smartville factory, club merchandise, and a whole lot more. The club's message boards are always busy, and its events always very well attended. It's a slick and efficient organisation by any standards.

The UK also boasts funkysmart, accessible via www.funkysmart.co.uk. This is another big smart club, this time with the emphasis very much on good times, a lively and entertaining website and major input from its members. Highlight of the year is an annual funkysmart gathering, attracting large numbers of club members and smart owners from all over the UK and beyond. It's a weekend of celebrating everything smart – and it's a great reason for joining the club and getting involved.

While the two main national clubs help to keep the British smart scene rolling, there's also a good selection of regional clubs dedicated to the marque – including midlandsmarts, northeast-smarts and sussexsmarts. Contact details of these and other UK-based clubs can be found in Appendix B.

Away from the major smart market in the UK, dedication to the brand is just as strong. Germany alone, for example, boasts upwards of 15 smart clubs, including national organisations, regional groups and even a couple of clubs dedicated solely to the roadster and roadster-coupé. The smart club scene in Germany is one of the most active in the world.

smart clubs in the rest of Europe also do well, and Appendix B includes online contact details for those in Switzerland, Italy, Spain, Greece, Sweden, Austria, The Netherlands and Belgium. We have

The biggest of its kind in the world, thesmartclub has been attracting an enthusiastic following since its formation in July 2000. (Author)

also managed to track down smart clubs in Mexico, Australia and even Taiwan, proof that the word about smart is continually spreading further. Why not check out their respective websites and get in touch, wherever you happen to live? The smart scene is very much an international one, and fellow owners always welcome contact from enthusiasts in other countries. Give it a try and you could find yourself with a whole load of new overseas friends to keep in touch with!

Many members of the various smart clubs also keep in touch with the whole scene via *smartimes*, a quarterly magazine published in Britain and dedicated to everything smart. It's available by subscription and mail order only, but it certainly fills a gap in the market and is avidly collected by increasing numbers of smart fanatics throughout the world. For details of how to get hold of a copy of *smartimes*, see the Specialists listings in Appendix B.

PUTTING ON A SHOW

Like any car brand with a strong club following, it is the smart social scene that's just as important to owners as any online activity. Whichever club you belong to, you should find plenty happening for you to take part in, ranging from monthly 'pub meets' and local get-togethers in your area, to major national and international shows and road runs.

The most famous example of the latter is the London to Brighton smart run organised by Britain's thesmartclub, in association with DaimlerChrysler UK. With widespread press and TV coverage, this has quickly established itself as one of the world's 'must see' smart extravaganzas and is renowned for attracting hundreds of owners of smarts of all types – from factory-standard examples to some of the weirdest and wackiest you're likely to find anywhere in Europe.

Like every other smart event, no matter what its size or scale, the emphasis here is on having a great time, meeting fellow owners and enthusiasts, getting yourself noticed and showing off your much-loved smart.

Can you think of another new car brand that attracts this much fanaticism, this much affection, this much enthusiasm, and this much club activity? smart owners know how to have a good time, and they certainly know how to get the most out of their ownership.

◤ Events like the annual London-to-Brighton smart run are a must-see experience for any smart owner or enthusiast. (Author)

◤ Wherever you live in the UK or throughout Europe, you will find plenty of smart get-togethers staged each summer. (Author)

▽ He'd never driven a
diesel smart before, but
that didn't stop Tony
Ormian ordering an
imported city-coupé cdi.
With slightly larger
capacity but a tad
less power, the cdi's
70mpg-plus is ample
compensation. (Author)

◪ **Dave and Claire Carter
have never regretted
leaving VW ownership
behind them. (Author)**

DAVE AND CLAIRE CARTER
CITY-COUPÉ PASSION

You'd expect the owners of a string of
Volkswagen Golf GTIs and a SEAT Ibiza GTI to stay
with the 'sporty VW' theme when they came to
change their car. But for 38-year-old Dave and 25-
year-old Claire, from Dudley in the West Midlands,
nothing could have been further from their minds.

'We were bored with the lack of character
offered by the latest VWs so we thought we'd go
for something completely different,' explains
Dave. That's why, at the beginning of 2004, they
opted for a nine-month-old smart city-coupé
passion. And they haven't looked back since.

'The only thing we argue about now is who's
going to drive the car,' laughs Claire. 'We both get
such a kick out of it, we can't wait to get behind
the wheel.'

The Carters' smart hasn't stayed standard, though. Since they bought it, they've invested in a Tuning Concepts re-map, a new dump valve, a K&N air filter and a modified tail pipe. With all this done, the car went on a rolling road and, to their delight, was found to be putting out 95bhp – a 50 per cent increase over standard.

'The turbo is real kick-in-the-pants stuff now,' says Dave. 'We had the 0–60mph time checked and confirmed recently at ten seconds dead – which we're really pleased with. Better than that, it actually feels a lot, lot faster. We've never had so much fun from a car before.'

TONY ORMIAN
CITY-COUPÉ CDI

April 2003 saw 58-year-old Tony Ormian investing in his second smart city-coupé. But instead of just popping down to his local smart centre, trading in his 2000 model and driving away in a brand-new replacement, he decided to do things differently:

'I'd never driven a diesel city-coupé before, but I was fascinated by the idea,' admits Tony, from Coventry. 'So I thought I'd take the plunge. The only trouble is, the cdi wasn't part of the official UK model range.'

Undeterred, Tony contacted independent importers cambridge smart cars and ordered a left-hand-drive city-coupé cdi, for the grand sum of £7,600. So has he encountered any difficulties switching to a diesel version?

'Not at all. In fact, I think it's fantastic. It sounds more or less the same as a petrol model, it feels almost as fast, but it gives me between 70 and 90 miles to each gallon. Hopefully it'll be very reliable, too; I know of another diesel that's done 175,000km (109,000 miles) so far, still on its original engine!'

The city-coupé cdi is a fairly rare model in the UK, having never been officially offered by smart. Happily though, Tony has no trouble getting it serviced or having any warranty work carried out at his nearest smart centre.

PHIL EGAN
ROADSTER

As the main organiser of midlandsmarts, a rapidly expanding group of smart fanatics based in central England, 25-year-old Phil is one of the biggest fans of the brand. So when he decided to get rid of his uprated city-coupé in 2003, what was he to replace it with?

'I managed to get hold of one of the last of the UK's left-hand-drive 61bhp roadsters that were being offered at the time for just £9,995,' boasts

Phil Egan is the organiser of midlandsmarts, and his 61bhp roadster was a bargain at less than £10k. (Author)

Useful mods and attractive colour-coding have transformed the roadster's looks. (Author)

The slogan beneath the numberplate is nicely self-deprecating… (Author)

Is there another city-coupé that attracts this much attention? Probably not. (Author)

It's obvious this particular smart fanatic is something of a patriot! (Author)

Phil. 'The forthcoming right-hand-drive models, with their extra power, were going to be a lot more expensive – so I didn't hesitate.'

Despite having a smaller turbo than most roadsters, Phil's example still has plenty of get-up-and-go. It looks great too, thanks to the new side skirts, boot spoiler, Compomotive wheels and general colour coding that Phil has invested in.

'I really like the new all-yellow look of my car,' admits Phil. 'It attracts lots of attention, too. The only thing I'd like to do now is perhaps lower the suspension a bit.'

IAN DOLPHIN
CITY-COUPÉ PULSE

Nobody could accuse smart owner Ian Dolphin of being a motoring introvert! His 2002-model city-coupé pulse is as patriotic as they come, thanks to panelwork adorned with the Union Flag. But Ian, from Gloucester, loves the attention it generates: 'It does stand out from the crowd, I must admit,' he says with a grin.

Apart from a set of eye-catching seven-spoke alloys, a smarts-R-us re-map, a K&N air filter and, of course, those fantastically eccentric body panels, Ian's city-coupé is fairly standard. But it attracts more interest out on the streets than just about anything else, particularly when Ian's sporting his own Union Flag baseball cap and matching T-shirt. Nobody would guess this most outgoing of smart enthusiasts actually drives a Daewoo every day…would they?

JILL FLYNN
CITY-COUPÉ

Here's a smart owner who just can't stop spending! After two years' ownership, 51-year-old Jill Flynn's city-coupé looks very, very different from when she first acquired it. And she probably hasn't finished yet…

Jill, from Burton-on-Trent, has so far invested in a smarts-R-us full body kit for wild head-turning looks, together with an engine re-map, new dump valve and uprated exhaust for added performance. The overall effect is startling – and Jill just can't get enough of it:

'I went to smarts-R-us to have a few jobs done and ended up spending a small fortune in their shop. Everything I saw on the shelves, I just had to have for my car,' she laughs. Watch out for Jill's very distinctive city-coupé at most of the UK's major smart events.

STEVE McMAHON
CITY-CABRIO

What does a former motorcyclist do when his wife persuades him to opt for something a bit safer?

▽ A smarts-R-us full body kit gives the city-coupé a whole new look. (Author)

▷ Spend, spend, spend! Jill Flynn loves adding to her collection of modifications. (Author)

From motorbike to city-cabrio – and just as much fun, reckons Steve McMahon. (Author)

Go out and buy a smart city-cabrio is the logical answer. That's what happened to 46-year-old Steve McMahon from Derbyshire:

'After a bad biking accident, I decided I'd had enough – I didn't want to put myself at risk any more. But I still wanted a plaything, something that would give me lots of fun out on the road to help soften the blow of no longer having a bike.'

For Steve, his 2003 city-cabrio – owned by him from new – is the next best thing to a motorbike: 'It's so much fun to drive, and the electric roof is a joy. The car was scratch black when I bought it, but I managed to acquire a set of yellow panels off a MkV for just £260 – so I tend to change the colour scheme with the seasons now. Yellow seems much more of a summery colour!

'I reckon I'll still have my cabrio in ten years time. It's a weekend fun car and should last indefinitely, I'm hoping. My family love it, too. It's so much more sociable than my old bike…'

ANNETTE HAYNES
CITY-COUPÉ

If you think it's a coincidence the surname Haynes appearing in a book from Haynes Publishing, it isn't. Annette Haynes is the wife of John Haynes OBE, founder and chairman of the publishing company – and she's also the very proud owner of her second city-coupé.

'I've had my little smart for quite a few years now,' explains Annette, 'and somehow I can't imagine life without it.' In fact, it's her vehicle of choice for most journeys, despite there being several other cars readily available to her.

'My husband does sometimes worry about me using the smart, though I don't know why,' she smiles. 'In fact, on one trip I had to make from our home in Somerset to London, I was determined to go in my smart – but John was only happy with this if I agreed to have our driver follow me all the way in the Mercedes! It was a strange situation, but I suppose it was quite reassuring. Needless to say, the smart behaved faultlessly.'

So what will Annette Haynes replace her city-coupé with when the time finally comes to part company? A new fortwo, of course. Like most smart owners, she's a total convert now.

MARTIN HUNT
ROADSTER

Ask 33-year-old Martin Hunt why he chose a roadster over a roadster-coupé and you're greeted with a wry smile: 'I didn't want to be bothered

Yellow body panels alternate with the original scratch black set. (Steve McMahon)

Despite the choice available to her, Annette Haynes often opts for the smart. (Haynes Publishing)

☐ He could have brought a BRABUS for the same money – but Martin Hunt's car is unique. (Author)

◪ The paint job is undoubtedly the most expensive modification here – but what a result! (Author)

▷ Yes, the city-coupé really is a small car… (Melanie Josling)

with the planning permission I'd need for the conservatory stuck on the back of the coupé!'

This is actually Martin's second roadster, even though it wasn't meant to be. He bought his first in October 2003 but experienced numerous problems with its traction control and ABS over the next few months. DaimlerChrysler couldn't sort the troubles for him, so they finally offered to swap the car for a new replacement in March '04. Fortunately, the second one has been a lot more reliable.

It also looks very different these days, thanks to an expensive respray in Rage Extreme Ecstasy, a set of BBS alloys, Eibach lowered (by 30mm) suspension and a restyled rear valance. Under the bonnet there's been a full re-map, along with a K&N air filter and stainless steel exhaust system. The end result is a fantastic looking machine with 108bhp at its disposal.

'I like to think of the roadster as a 21st century Fiat X1/9 – with extra performance and without the rust problems,' admits Martin, from Northumberland. An interesting comparison.

MELANIE JOSLING
CITY-COUPÉ PURE

If you're a fan of a certain bright orange cartoon cat going by the name of Garfield, you're not alone. Melanie Josling, from Somerset, shares the same passion, and you only have to glance at her smart city-coupé to realise this.

Melanie bought the car second-hand in 2003, but was never too happy with its red body panels; she wanted an orange smart that she could then adorn with Garfield decals and logos!

'I spent a few months collecting a spare set of body panels and then went to the paint shop to choose exactly the right shade – taking a toy Garfield with me,' recalls Melanie. 'The paint was matched and the panels were sprayed and swapped for the red ones. Then came the wheels – alloys or painted? I decided on painted, as they're far less common and I think they look better.'

Garfield decals were then ordered over the Internet, along with a whole range of Garfield-inspired interior adornments, including new car mats. But why Garfield? 'I just love his sense of humour,' explains Melanie. Fair enough.

FRODE MARTENS
CITY-COUPÉ

Despite the brand not being officially available in his native Norway, Frode Martens was determined to own a smart city-coupé back in 2001 – which is why he ended up buying an ex-German import, an early example manufactured in June 1999.

▽ In Norway, any smart city-coupé is a rare machine; Frode Martens' is an ex-German import. (Frode Martens)

▽ How's that for attention-grabbing signwriting? (Author)

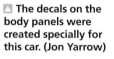
⬙ The decals on the body panels were created specially for this car. (Jon Yarrow)

Frode, now 41, a truck driver from Stavanger, still owns that same smart:

'When I first saw a smart, I decided there and then that I had to have one,' he confesses. 'I've loved my smart ever since and have never regretted buying it. Even when I had to replace the exhaust manifold recently, I didn't question my choice.'

Biggest problem is the 17-hour ferry trip to the UK to have his city-coupé serviced at an official smart centre. But even that doesn't deter Frode; neither does having to explain to his fellow Norwegians exactly what the car is: 'Nearly everyone I come across assumes it's an electric car, particularly as the electric-powered Think range – owned by Ford – used to be built in Norway!'

JON YARROW
CITY-COUPÉ PULSE

Back in 2000, while working in Munich, Jon Yarrow found himself amidst a whole load of smart enthusiasts, fast becoming addicted to what he calls 'smart culture'. And that was all it took. He returned home to Stratford upon Avon in 2001 and, before he knew it, had bought himself a new left-hand-drive city-coupé pulse.

Since then, Jon's smart has been treated to a set of Aluett alloys (purchased in Germany and brought back in the boot of the city-coupé), as well as a re-map to extract some extra performance.

Then there are the decals along the car's flanks, described by Jon as '…an ad hoc pattern of vinyl triangles designed to emulate the orange triangle in the original smart script'. A neat bit of detailing, and one that gives this particular city-coupé even more of an individual look.

Jon has also installed smart's official ISOFIX child safety seat system, enabling him to carry his young son around in complete safety.

IAN BOWER
FORTWO CABRIO PULSE

'Can you believe I used to own a Cadillac Coupe DeVille? Well, times they are a changing!' So says Ian Bower from Nottinghamshire, proud owner of this 2004 fortwo cabrio pulse. Since buying it new, Ian has invested in an engine re-map, an ICE upgrade and a full leather interior. But why the drastic change from a Cadillac to a smart?

'The first time I laid eyes on a smart I was transfixed,' he recollects. 'It had to be the cutest car on the planet.'

The driving experience is unbeatable too, he insists: 'When I'm driving my little smartie, with the top down and the wind in my hair, I still get an enormous smile on my face. People wave and smile back. I find myself going on trips just for the sake of it!'

⬙ The Aluett alloys, brought back from Germany, look fantastic. (Jon Yarrow)

JULIE BROOM
CITY-COUPÉ

Affectionately known as Grubby, Julie Broom's left-hand-drive city-coupé was registered in the UK in September 2001, having been imported from Belgium by an independent specialist.

Back then, Grubby was a standard bay grey model; now though, it looks drastically different, resplendent in aqua orange and complete with spoilers, side skirts and what its owner describes as '…various go-faster bits'.

Julie, from Newcastle upon Tyne, believes in making the most of Grubby: 'He used to have a reputation for not travelling too far from home,' she explains, 'but in 2004 he made his first trip back to the smart factory in France to see where he came from.'

◁ **You wouldn't expect an ex-Cadillac owner to fall for a smart fortwo, would you? (Ian Bower)**

△ Julie Broom's much-loved smart has gone from bay grey to aqua orange thanks to a panel swap. (Jason Revell)

▽ A simple faxed photograph started Anita Revell's obsession with all things smart. (Jason Revell)

◢ Affectionately known as Burdock, Anita Revell's city-coupé finally arrived on her birthday. (Jason Revell)

▷ If you can't beat 'em... Anita Revell's husband, Jason, has now joined the smart set. (Jason Revell)

It took five years for Emma Tysoe to finally get a smart of her own. (Emma Tysoe)

ANITA AND JASON REVELL
CITY-COUPÉS

When Anita Revell first heard about smart in 1999, she was more than a little curious: 'My job then involved arranging car rental and I found myself being asked to book smart cars in Paris and other European cities. Being naturally curious, I asked a rental company to fax a photo of a smart to me – and as soon as I saw it, I was besotted. I just had to have one…and so started two years of saving hard.'

Anita collected her city-coupé passion on her 31st birthday, back in 2001. It wasn't long before modifications started arriving in the shape of front and rear spoilers, non-standard alloys, uprated brakes, and a K&N air filter.

'I cover at least 13,000 miles a year in my smart now, and have visited the smartville factory in France on three different occasions.'

Anita's husband, Jason, soon fell for the smart life, too – and ended up buying himself a city-coupé: 'We both loved driving Anita's, so the only sensible option was for me to get one of my own,' he laughs.

'I really liked the aqua green panels I'd seen on some cars. They're quite rare, so when a set came up for sale I snapped them up – even though I hadn't yet found a car at that stage!'

Since then, Jason has acquired the city-coupé shown here, fitted the green panels and has

added an air scoop, alloys and bigger brakes. So is life with a pair of smarts idyllic? Very nearly, according to Jason: 'Yes, life is much better now that we have a smart each. But it does mean we usually have to get two sets of everything, and that means it can get expensive.'

EMMA TYSOE
CITY-COUPÉ

If patience is a virtue, Emma Tysoe must be one of the most virtuous individuals on the planet. She was a design student when she first heard that Swatch and Mercedes-Benz were working on a city car project with interchangeable body panels – and she fell in love with the concept straight away. Then, when she saw her first smart in 1998, she was hooked: 'I just adored the design and style – it was so cute.'

It wasn't until 2003 though, that Emma found herself in a position to buy a brand-new smart of her own. At last, her frustrating five-year wait was at an end.

These days, Emma runs her own origami business and has had her city-coupé sign-written to help promote it. But what about the future? 'My husband wants me to sell the car if we have a family, but I've said no – we'll just have one child so I can still use the smart, and when we go anywhere as a family we'll use his car.' So that's sorted then…

Some folk will go to any lengths to protect their smarts… (Emma Tysoe)

THE WEIRD AND
THE WONDERFUL

Any car that breaks a whole host of design barriers and creates an entirely new market segment for itself is, by definition, going to appeal to individualists. This is particularly true of the original smart city-coupé; nobody who likes blending into the background would ever consider buying such a unique machine. A rather useful knock-on effect of this is the potential for aftermarket accessories, modifications and upgrades.

No matter how successful the city-coupé was likely to prove, it was inevitable that a large proportion of its owners would want to make their cars just that little bit more special. They loved the individuality of their standard cars, but why stop there? Happily, the design and construction of the city-coupé means this is particularly easy compared with most other small cars, and it was only a matter of time before a whole new industry was created, catering purely for the needs of smart owners looking to make a difference.

PANEL ART

At the heart of the smart accessories and modifications market is, of course, smart GmbH themselves. Management at the company always knew this was an excellent way of starting to make money out of the brand early on, which is why smart now offer a vast array of aftermarket goodies – from replacement body panels to a wide range of branded clothing.

Although accessories and brightly coloured body panel packages were on offer very early on in the city-coupé's career, one of smart's most important launches occurred in December 2002,

when the 'smart individual' range was unveiled. By then, smart had seen for themselves how so many owners had personalised their cars' body panels with decals, airbrushing and – invariably – a great deal of imagination. So, with corporate tongue very firmly in cheek, out came a range of ten 'smart individual' body panel choices – ranging in design from zebra stripes, cheetah spots and a great white shark to bright red tomatoes, Scottish tartan and even the London skyline. No mainstream manufacturer had ever offered such an outrageous range of options before; once again, smart had succeeded in grabbing the motoring headlines.

So how were the city-coupé's panels altered in such a way? Robin Smart, spokesman for UK retailer smart Bluewater at the time, explained: 'The images are printed on heavy-duty vinyl which

▷ **How outrageous is this? smart became the only car manufacturer to offer cheetah spots and zebra stripes among its list of optional finishes. It cost from £1,500 in 2003. (Author)**

▽ **A subtle body kit and a set of big alloys were all that was needed to transform a standard city-coupe into this silver dream machine. (Author)**

Replacing a city-coupé or fortwo's plastic body panels is a relatively straightforward DIY job. Steve McMahon fancied a change from the original scratch black panels of his city-cabrio. (Steve McMahon)

The old ones are off and the new ones are ready to be fitted. Yellow replacement panels will transform the look of Steve's car. (Steve McMahon)

◁ **Almost finished! With the panels replaced and just the exterior trim to refit, it now looks like a completely different vehicle. Second-hand panels in this instance made the whole thing very cost-effective. (Steve McMahon)**

is then wrapped and stuck on the removable body panels. We have come up with a number of designs – but smart drivers don't have to let their imagination stop there. If they have a suitable image, we can put anything on the cars.'

Prices in the UK at the time started at around £1,500 to design, print and fit the vinyl to any city-coupé's panels; or customers could buy a brand-new 'smart individual' city-coupé from £8,695. The 'individual' format certainly added a fair chunk to the cost of any smart, which meant many owners went for less expensive options.

The beauty of the city-coupé's TRIDION-based design was that the plastic body panels attached to it have always been easily removable and replaceable. It's one of the great advantages of the model as a city-based commuter car. After a minor bump or an experience with careless trolley-pushers on any supermarket car park, it's simplicity itself to remove and replace any damaged body panel with another. It also means, of course, that if you get fed up with the panel colour of your city-coupé or fortwo, you can pop down to your nearest smart centre and order a full replacement set in another colour. It's a quick and straightforward way of giving your car a whole new look; it could even fool your neighbours into thinking you've bought a new car!

smart have always been keen to make the most of this market, which is why you'll find body panel packages in all sorts of different colours – from standard hues like lite white, phat red and jack black, through a range of metallics (including star blue and bay grey), and on to more imaginative choices like numeric blue and scratch black with their truly un-standard look.

For many owners, of course, such a choice simply isn't enough. They don't just want their cars to be different; they want them to be positively unique. That's why many enthusiasts have their own livery, decals, vinyl and designs applied to their cars, often employing the services of a local signwriter to help them out. The end results range from the bizarre to the fantastic, with just about every other adjective imaginable in between. From national flags to fruit, corporate logos to seascapes, the opportunities are limitless. Yes, owning an affordable and economical car has never been a more individual experience.

△ **Some people will go to any lengths to make their smart stand out in a crowd! National flags are a particularly popular way of personalising city-coupés and fortwos. (Author)**

But what about those owners who want to give their city-coupés and fortwos a bit more 'attitude'? Fear not, because there are smart specialists who offer a good choice of spoilers, side skirts and full body kits to make any example that bit more sporting – and macho.

One of Europe's biggest suppliers of such kits is the UK's smarts-R-us, based in Nottingham and offering a great range of merchandise, including their own body kits. You can buy individual items or complete kits, depending on your personal preferences. Either way, it's a superb and relatively simple way of trans-forming an innocent looking city-coupé or fortwo into a mean and moody creation that any Citroën Saxo-driving 20-year-old would be proud to be seen in.

THE OFFICIAL LINE

Even if replacing the body panels isn't part of your smart-owning master plan, your nearest smart centre will still be able to relieve you of some more of your hard-earned cash. That's because they offer a large array of add-ons, goodies and merchandise designed to make you wonder how you ever survived without them. In the case of the city-coupé and fortwo, these range from bike

◬ Replacement body panels in numeric blue, scratch black and aqua orange have managed to transform the appearance of these three city-coupés. It's an affordable way of giving your smart a new lease of life – particularly if it has become the victim of parking knocks and grazes over the years. (Author)

racks, wheel trims and alloys to child seats, ICE upgrades, and sports exhausts.

For proud owners who like to wear what they drive, smart also offers the extensive smartware range, comprising clothing, personal accessories, baggage and even stuff for the kids. So whether it's a T-shirt, a weekend bag, a radio-controlled fortwo or a smart umbrella that you simply can't manage without, a visit to any smart centre is the answer to your prayers.

Buyers of new roadsters, roadster-coupés and forfours are as well catered for when it comes to accessories and optional extras as the owners of the smaller smarts. Again, a healthy line-up of alloys, bigger and better ICE, various safety enhancements and even full leather trim are all available when you order your new smart – assuming you've got the funds to pay for them, of course.

▽ **It's a 'his and hers' smart – but guess who gets to drive it most! The graphics on this particular city-coupé raise a smile wherever it goes. Perfect for cruising the seafront at Newquay or Brighton… (Author)**

Anyone who buys a smart isn't afraid to go their own way – and the company's official range of optional extras, accessories and merchandise makes sure of this.

THE BEAUTY OF BRABUS

We've already looked at how tuning specialists BRABUS transformed the roadster and roadster-coupé (see Chapter Four) when they got their expert hands on them. But there's far more to BRABUS's involvement in smart than those two sportsters.

The name BRABUS has long been associated with go-faster Mercedes-Benz models. This merry band of German engineering experts has built some of the most impressive high-powered executive saloons and sports cars over the years, all of them using Mercedes models as their basis. It was only a matter of time before they officially

△ **With the right kind of logos and lettering, your city-coupé can be transformed into an eye-catching runabout that also does a marvellous job of advertising your business. It's a miniature billboard on wheels! (Author)**

▽ **Pick your own! Fruit – in this case, strawberries – is another popular choice for the smart owner desperate to display some individualism. Once you've got your hands on a set of suitable decals, it's a simple enough change of image. (Author)**

got to grips with creating more powerful smarts – which they did, culminating in the creation of smart-BRABUS GmbH in March 2002.

With ownership of the company split 50/50 between MCC smart GmbH (as it was still then known) and BRABUS GmbH, this was very much a joint venture. The first priority of the new concern was to go further with the city-coupé than smart themselves had so far dared.

Official BRABUS versions of the city-coupé went on sale, looking magnificent thanks to their BRABUS-designed body kits, and offering extra performance and handling thanks to the engineering changes that had gone on under the skin. The main point about those showroom-ready BRABUS city-coupés though, was to show just what was available from the extensive new range of BRABUS accessories and upgrades. Relatively few buyers would choose the mightily expensive full BRABUS package, to be honest, but

at least the availability of the ready-made BRABUS city-coupé provided a useful 'menu' from which buyers could choose whichever modifications they either desired or could afford.

In their road test of the new smart BRABUS in January 2003, Britain's *Auto Express* magazine reported: 'The accessories certainly make it more aggressive, with a front end that now resembles a snowplough and a more attractive rear, with centrally mounted twin exhaust pipes. BRABUS wheels are another welcome addition, giving the car a healthy dose of style, but making the smart's ride even worse thanks to ultra-low-profile tyres.'

Auto Express was full of praise for the new paddle-shift gearchange developed for the BRABUS model, but not so enthusiastic about the power boost, created by modifications to the turbocharger and engine management system: 'The engine has been upgraded to deliver an extra 9bhp, taking the total to 70bhp, but you'd be

◳ **Known as the smart Sweet Chariot, this amazing city-coupé was created by smart of Nottingham and smart of Derby to celebrate England's historic win in the 2003 Rugby World Cup. It featured the signature of every team member, including coach Sir Clive Woodward. The car was subsequently sold at auction to raise money for the BBC's Children In Need appeal. (smart East Midlands)**

hard pushed to tell the difference this makes, as the smart's limited pace is hardly altered. Acceleration is still modest…'

It wasn't necessarily that magazines like *Auto Express* didn't understand the concept of the BRABUS package; more that they seemed to think it was expensive for what it achieved, with even just the BRABUS body kit costing the best part of £3,000 in the UK in 2003. In fact, a fully loaded smart BRABUS with everything available specified would end up costing its buyer more than twice as much as a standard, entry-level city-coupé pure. Even so, that didn't mean *Auto Express* was completely dismissive in their summing-up of the BRABUS: 'You'll either love or loathe the smart BRABUS. Whether you see it as a tasteless styling conversion or a performance city car, one thing is certain – kitting it out can be expensive. Thankfully, you can pick and choose individual items, keeping the cost down.'

▽ From alloys to baseball caps, stereos to jumpers, the accessories and smartware ranges offer a vast selection to keep the real aficionados happy. (Author)

△ If you thought the city-coupé and fortwo couldn't get any smaller, think again. smart centres stock a good selection of radio-controlled models, as well as miniature roadsters. (Author)

And that seemed to be the key to BRABUS's future success with smart. You only have to glance through a current brochure for the fortwo, roadster or forfour to find a good selection of BRABUS-branded accessories and upgrades available. Again, any smart centre will provide you with the latest prices and specifications for the model you're interested in. In essence though, whatever it is you're looking for when personalising or improving your smart, there'll be a BRABUS solution available to you.

ANOTHER WAY

◣ Many smart specialists offer body kits and various restyling accessories. One of the most popular is the full kit from Britain's smarts-R-us, shown here. This is a city-coupé with real attitude! (Author)

◩ The official smart bike rack is an impressive piece of kit, even with the bike missing! All official smart accessories are designed with style very much in mind. (Author)

Increasing numbers of smart owners though, are now looking away from the official smart and BRABUS scene, focussing instead on the independent specialists that can be found scattered throughout Europe. In the two major smart markets that are Germany and Britain, there's no shortage of such companies.

Names well known to smart enthusiasts in the UK include smarts-R-us, smart tune and smart store. Other companies exist that can also help, and a comprehensive listing appears in Appendix B.

smarts-R-us, in particular, has established itself as a major supplier of smart parts and accessories, with a vast choice of interior and exterior cosmetic enhancements available, as well as mechanical and electronic upgrades. The company's ECU re-mapping service is particularly popular, enabling owners to boost the power of their city-coupés, fortwos and roadsters without spending a fortune – in fact, less than £300 at the time of writing. Also popular are new dump valves (which means extra power and a fantastic 'whooshing' sound when the turbo's hard at work – great for the show-offs among us!), induction kits, performance exhausts and Eibach stiffened suspension.

Just about all the service and maintenance parts you're ever likely to need are available, too. smarts-R-us has also established a joint venture with a leading German engine remanufacturer to supply fully reconditioned 600cc smart engines, warranted and available from stock from £799, in 2004.

Check out the websites of all the UK-based

◁ The BRABUS city-coupé came as standard with a 70bhp version of the three-cylinder engine, later upgraded to 74bhp. It provided a useful increase in performance, although no more than many owners, who have since invested in an ECU re-map, have come to expect. (smart UK)

smart specialists listed in Appendix B for full details of exactly what's on offer. But, wherever you live and whatever type of smart you own, don't forget the many specialists based in mainland Europe, too. Just because a smart specialist happens to be in another country doesn't mean they won't be able to help you – and they may well offer items that you can't find more locally.

Companies such as Germany's SW-Exclusive, parts4smarts, smartspeed and Lumma Tuning all offer a great choice of styling and tuning parts and accessories for most smart models.

It's also worth mentioning Opera Design, based in Laupheim, Germany, which design and produce their own extensive range of styling modifications for smarts – as well as various Mercedes models. (How do you fancy a Mercedes SL with a gullwing door conversion? Hmmm…) It's worth checking out their fascinating website (available with German or English text) just to get an idea of what's available for smarts; I think you'll be surprised at the impressive array of goodies on offer and delivery anywhere in Europe shouldn't be a problem.

WORDS OF WARNING

What's particularly interesting about a large proportion of smart owners who start modifying their cars is that they've never considered doing this with any of their previous vehicles. So many folk driving around in modified city-coupés and fortwos wouldn't have dreamt of spending money on add-ons, mods and upgrades before – so why now?

Part of the reason, perhaps, is the kid-in-a-sweetshop syndrome; there's such a wide range of worthwhile stuff on the market these days specifically for smarts that it's hard for any owner to resist. Then there's the simplicity of it all; smarts are among the easiest cars to modify, and you don't need to spend a fortune in order to see

The fully kitted-out BRABUS city-coupé and city-cabrio models were seriously expensive by smart standards. A fully loaded example could cost at least twice as much as an entry-level city-coupé pure in 2003. (smart UK)

△ For the smart fanatic who wants the ultimate and doesn't mind paying for it, BRABUS offers a good choice of upgrades and accessories. Shown here is a city-coupé passion adorned with BRABUS goodies. (smart UK)

some very tangible results.

So are there any drawbacks to modifying your smart – and is there anything you need to beware of before you start? The best advice is to stick with the people who know what they're talking about – and that means the most highly respected specialists on the scene.

Talk to fellow members of thesmartclub or funkysmart (either in person or via the clubs' online message boards – there's always somebody willing to help) about what you're trying to achieve. Do you want extra power? Better handling? A cool body kit? Whatever it is, there are always lots of suggestions available at the click of a mouse.

Most popular methods of achieving extra brake-horsepower include the re-mapping of your ECU, fitting a dump valve and investing in a K&N air filter. These changes alone will add anything up to 50 per cent to the power output of your city-coupé or fortwo. But make sure you have any

such work carried out by a reputable smart specialist who has done plenty of similar conversions. The good news is that these mods seem not to have any major effect on the longevity and reliability of smart's tiny three-pot motor.

When it comes to improving the handling and grip of your smart, you've got various options. Stiffer springs from the likes of Eibach will mean less roll when cornering at speed, and giving the car a more confident feel in the process – but they can also mean an even harsher ride.

The same applies when upgrading wheel and tyre sizes, with many owners choosing to fit larger fronts in particular; this can improve handling at the limit, while having the unexpected side-effect of lighter steering, too. A harsher ride is one consequence you might not be happy with however.

The best advice is: seek advice. There are so

Europe has a good choice of independent smart specialists offering a wide array of parts, accessories and upgrades – and most of them provide Internet shopping via their various websites. Such temptation… (Author)

Every smart and its various derivatives eventually finds itself at the hands of tuners, modifiers and fanatical owners. How far you choose to take such modifications though, will depend on your personal taste – and the depth of your pockets. (Author)

Side skirts, a front spoiler and a set of stylish new panels make any city-coupé a head-turning machine, no matter what it looked like before. (Author)

many enthusiastic smart owners out there in clubland who will be more than willing to share their experiences. The same applies to the best of the specialists who, once you've discussed your available budget, will be able to explain the most effective modifications for your particular needs.

On the cosmetic side, decisions are based more around personal preferences. Not everyone likes the same body kit, spoiler or set of panels, so it's a subjective choice and one that can be as individual and creative as you are. Even without going to the extent of a complete body kit, the simple additions of a new front grille, chrome petrol cap cover, chrome stoneguard and perhaps a front 'bull bar' will give your city-coupé or fortwo a distinctive new look. All this is easy to fit, and won't cost you a fortune to buy in the first place.

How far you go with your cosmetics is therefore your decision, but how much difference will such mods make to your smart's insurance cover and premium? The legal standpoint is that any changes you make to your car's standard specification should be notified to your insurers, and, to be honest, that's the best advice. There's little point investing in an expensive set of alloys if they're not covered on your insurance simply because you didn't inform your insurance company of the change.

With any tuning mods too, the advice has to be: keep them informed. Boosting the power of

your smart without your insurers being aware could technically mean – in the event of an accident or claim – that you don't actually have any valid cover. Not only is that then illegal, but it could prove to be a very costly mistake on your part.

The good news is that as long as any modifications to your car have been carried out by a reputable smart specialist to a high standard, they should add relatively little to your insurance premium. Even better is that many such mods don't even cause problems with your official manufacturer's warranty, though it's worth checking this out at your nearest smart centre before you proceed.

One last point here, this time – in the case of the UK – is about the DVLA. Newcomers to the smart brand might assume that every time they change the colour of their body panels, they need to notify DVLA of this and arrange for a new Registration Document to be issued. But, actually, this isn't the case. The colour of your smart is judged solely by the colour of its TRIDION safety cell – so you can change the colour of your car as many times as you like and not have to worry about contacting the boffins at Swansea. It's probably a good job really; otherwise, just how would you describe the colour of a smart clad with cheetah-style spots or enormous strawberries on its panels? How indeed.

You want to improve your brakes, get some extra power, create better handling and make your smart stand out in a crowd? Then make sure you talk to people who've already done similar things before you part with your hard-earned cash. Their advice can be invaluable; there's plenty of help out there if you ask. (Author)

BUYING
A SMART

Despite being Europe's youngest major car brand, smart has been around long enough now for potential buyers to get an idea of its overall reliability. The oldest city-coupés, on which this can be judged, are those produced in the summer of 1998 for the European launch that autumn. It must be stressed though, that with innumerable improvements made over the years, the robustness and dependability of later examples is even more impressive. It is one of those classic situations where it pays to buy the best and latest example you can afford – assuming you're buying second-hand, of course.

Buying a brand-new smart couldn't be easier. You either pop along to one of the world's many smart centres, talk to the staff, browse the accessories catalogue and place your order; or you log on to the smart website relevant to your country and do the whole thing online. smart was the first European car brand to offer full Internet buying facilities, enabling customers to order the smart of their choice by credit card and then have delivery to their door once the vehicle was ready. Buying a new smart has always been a straightforward process, the most complicated part being your final choice of exact specification.

But what about the used smart scene? For a start, should potential owners only ever buy a second-hand smart from an official smart centre?

WHERE TO BUY

Now that smart has been around for some time, you'd expect large numbers of the city-coupé, in particular, to be available from outside the official dealer network by now. And, yes, they are

there – but perhaps not in the numbers you'd expect.

What smart has managed to achieve during its first few years on sale is the most amazing level of customer loyalty – something that most rival manufacturers can only dream of. In these days of money-saving promotions, special offers and customer incentives, brand loyalty from car buyers is rapidly becoming a thing of the past for most mainstream manufacturers; people will now chop and change their favoured car marque with the kind of regularity not experienced twenty or thirty years ago. Happily though, smart is one of the few exceptions to this rule.

The inevitable result of this is a good choice of used smarts at all smart centres, as existing owners part-exchange their current models for one a bit newer or a tad different. Pay a visit to any smart centre in any market and you'll find not only a great choice of used smarts, but just about all of

▶ **Thanks to unprecedented levels of loyalty towards the smart brand, you'll find a fantastic choice of part-exchanged used cars at your nearest smart centre. They can pack a lot of smarts onto a single forecourt! (Author)**

▽ **You want to buy a brand-new smart? You don't even need to visit a smart centre in order to do so. smart was the first major marque to offer full online car-buying facilities – all at the click of a mouse. (Author)**

pint size fun, full size drive

them will have been 'swapped' for another smart as part of a trade-in. At the very least, this should act as an encouragement to first-time buyers of the brand; if a customer is happy enough with their smart to go out and buy another, surely their old one will be worth snapping up second-hand?

Of course, smart centres aren't the only source of used cars. You'll also find smarts advertised privately in many motoring magazines and car sales publications. In the UK, for example, a search through the weekly *AutoTrader* or a glance at their website (www.autotrader.co.uk) will usually bring up a list of smart cars advertised privately. There's absolutely no reason why such vehicles won't be good buys, particularly if they're under three years old and still covered by the original manufacturer's warranty. You may even be able to save some money buying this way, as private sales tend to undercut dealer prices by some margin. Inevitably though, it's a more complicated way of buying, as you could end up travelling hundreds of miles just to view a handful of smarts for sale privately. When it comes to sheer convenience

◁ **The slogan says it all. Fun is such a rare commodity in today's increasingly bland car market. (Author)**

WHAT THE PRESS SAID: BUYING A CITY-COUPÉ

'If you have a tendency to lose things, then the smart car may not be for you. Now you wouldn't think that it's possible to lose a car, but the smart is so small that unless you can remember where you parked it, it may take you a while to find. OK, now you can rule out the back of the sofa, because it's too big to take refuge with the money, the remotes and the like – but if you're trying to find one in a busy supermarket car park, it can do a remarkable impression of Shergar. "Now I'm sure I left it there – oh no, that's a supermarket trolley." Once a rare sight on our roads, more and more of the little devils seem to be appearing ... it's no wonder, because in a world of car design devoid of character, the smart is a refreshing breath of fresh air.'

Top Gear magazine (UK), February 2001

and a decent choice, there's little to touch a smart centre.

Used smarts are also cropping up these days at other (non-smart) franchised dealers throughout Europe, most of them the result of those rare occasions when existing owners part-exchange their vehicles for another brand. It's therefore not unheard of to see city-coupés and fortwos for sale at Fiat, Citroën or Peugeot dealers – perhaps because their owners have traded up to larger four-seaters like the Punto, C2 or 206. Check out the full history of the smart and talk to the salesman about why the owner changed brands – perhaps even contacting the owner direct, via their details on the Registration Document. It always pays to make sure they were generally happy with their car before you become its second (or third, or fourth) owner.

Older examples of the city-coupé can even be found nowadays at some of the smaller used-car-only garages throughout Europe, which is not necessarily a bad thing. A five or six-year-old smart will, by now, be too aged for either a smart centre or a non-smart franchised dealer to have on their forecourt, as most companies tend to have an 'up-to-three-years-only' policy on the age of their stock. Older smarts will therefore get passed on through the trade or via car auctions, usually ending up in the hands of used car dealers as a result. Many dealers specialising in older cars formerly steered well clear of used smarts, fearful of their technology and what might go wrong and need putting right; now though, they're beginning to realise that a smart on their forecourt can be quite an asset – and should sell easily. It's good news, as it gives the buyers of older smarts far greater choice in terms of where to find them.

BUYER BEWARE

Wherever you're buying from though, and no matter what model of smart you're looking at or how old it is, there are some basic checks you should carry out before you consider parting with your cash. At the best of times, buying a used car is a minefield of dangers and pitfalls; and when you see a smart that seems exactly what you've been searching high and low for, it's so easy to get carried away in the excitement and forget some

▶ You do see smarts advertised privately these days, as well as through non-franchised dealers. Sometimes it's a cheaper option than buying from a smart centre – but not always. (Author)

basic procedures. That's when you're particularly vulnerable.

So, for a start, when buying any used smart, only ever arrange to meet the vendor at their own home or (in the case of a dealer) at their premises. Meeting 'halfway' or arranging to have the car brought to your address is a classic ploy used by sellers who don't actually own the vehicles in question.

If buying privately, remember this: when you get to the vendor's house, ask to see the vehicle's Registration Document (or its equivalent in non-UK countries) and check that the seller's name and the address shown on the V5C correspond with where you actually are. If you've any doubts or concerns, simply walk away. If there is no V5C offered with the vehicle at all ('I haven't long moved house and the log book's still at DVLA,' the vendor may claim), don't buy the car under any circumstances, no matter how tempting it seems.

Checking the genuineness of a vehicle goes much further, though. Still with the Registration Document in your hand, take a look at the smart's VIN number; check it with the number that's printed on the document and, if there's any discrepancy whatsoever, don't even consider buying the car. It's that simple.

At this stage, you also need to be looking into the smart's history, to check that what the vendor claims to be a full-service history actually is, as well as using this to help verify the mileage. Never accept a vendor's claim that '…the service book is still at the garage; I forgot to pick it up when I had the car serviced last week.' If a service history is boasted about, you want to be able to see it in front of you before you even consider making an offer.

Don't be afraid to spend time carefully studying the service book and any previous MoT certificates that are with the smart, too. Check that all the mileages shown on certain dates seem to tally with what's being claimed about the vehicle. You might even want to make a note of the previous owner's name and address, approaching them before you hand over any money, to ensure they can back up what you've been told and vouch for the car's history.

Another obvious point when viewing any used

car is to look for signs of a forced entry, which relates to the previous point about checking out the vendor's actual ownership. It's a sad fact of life that many thousands of cars get broken into each year, so any signs of a previous break-in may simply have occurred during the current keeper's ownership; don't be afraid to ask, because there's no reason why they should hide this from you. If, however, you can clearly see that a door lock has been forced or you can see signs of shattered glass inside the car, you have every right for your

WHAT THE PRESS SAID: BUYING A CITY-COUPÉ

'The smart is proving to be extremely resilient in the marketplace, even in left-hand drive form, says trade bible Glass's Guide. Part of its success lies in its clever promotion, as premium market customers see it as a Mercedes. With further brand expansion on the way, there's no reason to suspect a decline in demand or popularity of the smart. Cabriolets and passion models hold their value best.'

Auto Express magazine (UK), March 2003

▽ Second-hand smarts represent great value. Whatever the price, age and location of the car though, always carry out the same basic checks before you part with your money. (Author)

◁ Once the forfour was finally on sale, owners of city-coupés like these who suddenly needed four seats, could now remain loyal to the smart brand. (Author)

suspicions to be aroused when the vendor denies all knowledge.

HISTORY LESSON

The subject of any smart's service history, as mentioned earlier, is an important one for all potential owners to bear in mind. For a start, it offers some kind of reassurance that the smart you're interested in has been both maintained properly and reasonably well looked after. Just as important though, it should confirm whether the car has been the subject of various smart recalls over the years.

Official recalls tended to affect only the earlier

smarts – an indication of how improved the products have been in more recent times. Back in 2000, for example, smart began contacting existing owners of city-coupés to ask them to take their vehicles for a safety check of the TRUST-PLUS software system – involving an examination of the carrier links on the front axle and on the throttle pedal module. Very few cars experienced problems, but those that did should have had replacement components fitted free of charge; and, in most cases, there should be a record of this in the car's service history.

Other official recalls over the years have focussed on the city-coupé's engine idle speed (requiring a replacement pedal moulding

◁ Manufacturers don't like official recalls – they cost money and spoil reputations. Fortunately, smart's recalls affected mainly the earliest city-coupés, rather than later examples like this. (Author)

equipped with a safety return spring) and the effectiveness of the engine drive-train control (which necessitated re-programming). There's also been a recall in connection with possible water penetration of the front suspension ball joint, resulting in replacement ball joints being fitted to affected vehicles.

Most such recalls have involved only city-coupés built in 1998 and '99, with various design and engineering changes helping to prevent such problems on later vehicles. If you're intent on buying a pre-2000 city-coupé though, it's worth ensuring – via the service history or through smart itself – that it has had any necessary checks and remedial work carried out. If in any doubt, simply find another smart to buy.

Official recalls are never popular with car manufacturers; they cost a lot of money and they can bring about some negative publicity. But they're a fact of life with so many new models, often from some of the world's most prestigious car manufacturers. Don't let the number of smart recalls during the marque's earlier days deter you from buying into the brand now; things have improved greatly since then. And anyway, most recalls are precautionary only, with relatively few vehicles actually affected in most cases. smart is no different to any other brand in that respect.

FAULTS AND FOIBLES

This doesn't mean that life with a second-hand smart is entirely joyful or problem-free, though. Like any used car, faults can arise and frustration can ensue. One annoying problem with the very earliest city-coupés, for example, was a tendency for their heated rear window elements to get too hot and for the glass to shatter as a result. Most rear screens on 1998 and '99 city-coupés have since been replaced (featuring curved heating elements instead of the previous straight ones), which means it's no longer an issue in those cases. However, it does highlight the fact that no car is perfect – and the first of those smallest smarts were no exception.

It is also worth paying attention to a city-coupé's handbrake before you buy. This has never been one of smart's strongest points, and it's not unknown for the handbrake to fail to engage on

Are you concerned about the car's history? Does what the vendor tells you really add up? Have certain items been strangely replaced without explanation? Checking the genuineness of any smart – whatever its age – is essential. (Author)

WHAT THE PRESS SAID:
BUYING A ROADSTER-COUPÉ

'Legroom is excellent and the driving position is as good as in LHD variants, although large drivers may find the lack of space between their legs and the steering wheel a problem. Other irritations include a hopelessly small glove compartment and narrow door pockets. But you'll forgive the coupé these vices as soon as you fire up the perky three-cylinder engine.'

Auto Express magazine (UK),
September 2003

early right-hand-drive (2001) models. Again, many examples have had modifications carried out to cure this, and it's worth asking about this if you're buying an early right-hooker. Otherwise, just make sure the handbrake is working effectively and is capable of holding the car on a steep incline.

Another annoying fault centred around the city-coupé's indicator and lights stalk. Bizarrely, if the interior light stopped working in some examples, it also meant the car's tail lights went out – even though the bulbs were fine. It's a simple job to swap a faulty stalk and your nearest smart centre will be able to advise on this.

It needs to be mentioned that a 'bad batch' of

city-coupé fuel tanks cropped up mainly during Mk5 production, which means some cars show 'empty' on their fuel gauges even though there's still five or more litres in the tank. It might not sound too inconvenient, but in a car with just a 22-litre petrol tank it can be frustrating!

Rather more serious was a problem with the exhaust manifold on pre-2001 smarts, which meant it was prone to cracking – sometimes after just 20–30,000 miles. For any owner whose car was then out of warranty, it meant a big bill and an equally large headache. By the time the Mk6 city-coupé arrived, the problem had been dealt with thanks to a redesigned manifold.

Generally though, smart's Mercedes-developed three-cylinder Suprex engine is a reliable and trustworthy little lump. As the years have passed and the average mileage of older smarts has increased, the in-built reliability has shone through. Despite their tiny stature and their high-revving nature, these powerplants aren't renowned for any major problems. Even so, it's important to carry out some basic checks – including signs of any water in the engine oil (is there any white 'gunk' around the oil filler neck?), which might suggest head gasket problems. You also need to check for a smooth, even tickover – although erratic idling is more likely to be an electrical or electronic matter rather than any serious engine fault.

Despite the engine's basic reliability, it is usually advisable to buy the lowest-mileage city-coupé,

▽ This very early example of a city-coupé still has its original rear screen – complete with straight heated rear window elements which, in some cases, caused the window to shatter. This should have been changed via an official recall. (Author)

WHAT THE PRESS SAID: BUYING A FORTWO

'It might have received a relatively muted response from the public when it was first launched, but the diminutive smart has slowly taken hold of the public's consciousness and is now a familiar sight around towns and cities. Now it's not just visible around city centres – the smart has gone all suburban, being bought as a second car for families or a first car to younger buyers.'

Auto Express magazine (UK), June 2004

◨ Post-2001 city-coupés featured a modified exhaust manifold, a response to a problem with cracking on earlier examples. Generally though, any three-cylinder Suprex engine is a reliable unit, even after a high mileage. (Author)

fortwo or roadster you can afford – depending, of course, on the size of your budget. Not only will this help to ensure the most reliable motoring for your money, it will also make resale easier later on; you may trust a high-mileage Suprex engine, but will your potential buyers feel the same in a year or two's time?

Remember, too, that smart's original warranty offering in most markets was for a maximum of three years or 25,000 miles (40,000km) – whichever came sooner. It would be easy to assume this means a smart engine is past its best at 25,000-plus, even though history now shows us this simply isn't the case; nevertheless, it doesn't stop potential buyers from making such an assumption. Incidentally, smart's warranty was

altered in January 2002, to offer two years of unlimited mileage cover and a six-year anti-corrosion guarantee; the new 'unlimited mileage' aspect helped to send out a new, more positive message to potential buyers.

Interestingly, at the time of writing, there has been some discussion on the message board of www.funkysmart.co.uk regarding high-mileage city-coupés and fortwos, with one member covering 32,000 miles in his first year of fortwo ownership. He was concerned he was expecting too much from his car, and asked fellow members for advice. The overwhelming response was encouraging, with several members citing city-coupés with upwards of 100,000 miles recorded so far – all with few problems. It seems there are many smart owners out there who think nothing of piling on the miles very quickly.

It is equally good news when it comes to a smart's gearbox. Despite its hi-tech design, this sequential-style semi-automatic transmission is relatively rugged in everyday use. Serious problems are rare, and transmission-based warranty claims pretty unusual. Even so, before you buy the used smart of your choice, make sure you drive it extensively in both fully automatic and semi-auto settings. Does the semi-auto set-up select the gear you want within less than a second? Are all six gears useable in both transmission settings? Take a long test drive on a variety of roads, up and down different inclines and at a whole range of different speeds to fully satisfy yourself that the gearbox and automatic clutch mechanisms are working as smart intended. If in any doubt whatsoever, get a smart centre or independent vehicle examiner to check it out for you.

You need to apply the same degree of common sense, too, when it comes to areas like a smart's anti-lock braking system. Is it working as it should? Do the brakes pull the car up quickly and in a straight line? Can you detect the ABS activating itself on damp roads? Again, this should all be part of any test drive you take in a second-hand smart.

The easiest way to achieve peace of mind, of course, is to buy a smart that's still covered by its original manufacturer's warranty – in terms of both age and mileage. If the car you're interested

◁ **Check on any smart that the ABS system is still fully functioning and that, on later models, the traction control set-up is as it should be. Any used-car warranty should cover these areas, but it always pays to read the small print. (Author)**

WHAT THE PRESS SAID: BUYING A FORFOUR

'If the name suggests a certain Ronseal 'does what it says on the tin' simplicity, then here's another word to ponder on: premium. Prosperous and clever people buy smarts apparently, and spec their cars accordingly (especially in the UK). No surprise, then, that the new MINI is the forfour's chief touchstone, with the Peugeot 206 and VW Polo as secondary rivals.'

Top Gear magazine (UK), April 2004

in is approaching its third birthday or has even gone beyond it, you should be able to negotiate for a warranty if you're buying from a dealer; be aware though, that there are far more exclusions in a used-car warranty than in smart's original, and you may find most potential faults being put down to simple 'wear and tear' and therefore not covered. It always pays to read the small print.

An area of any smart that is rather easier for which to ascertain the condition is, not unexpectedly, its bodywork. With the roadster, roadster-coupé and forfour still being relatively new models in most markets, bodywork problems on used examples are likely to be few and far between, but both the fortwo and the city-coupé before it are prone to certain areas of damage.

COSMETIC HELP

The good news, of course, is that the smart city-coupé's original design and method of construction means traditional bodywork problems of rust, stone chips and minor accident damage are either done away with or are certainly easier to put right when they do occur.

Take the subject of rust. It's a well known fact that modern cars rust at a far slower rate than their counterparts of three decades ago; in the 1970s it wasn't unusual for a Cortina or Marina to be merrily rusting away by the time it reached its fifth birthday, while most cars of the 1990s onwards fair rather better than this. Even so, the good folk at smart decided to take things a step further and, thanks to the innovative TRIDION safety cell and plastic panel idea detailed in Chapter Two, created a range of cars with none of the traditional bodywork woes. The TRIDION safety cell itself, for example, is powder coated and very robust – and is unlikely to suffer from any kind of structural corrosion even in old age.

As for the plastic body panels that help to give so many smarts their wacky appearance … well, these are quickly and easily interchangeable, either as complete sets or as individual panels. Once a smart has accumulated its fair share of parking knocks and shopping trolley grazes, it's simple enough to give your city-coupé or fortwo a whole new look with a brand-new set of panels – in any of the wide range of colours available.

▶ Pay attention to a second-hand smart's wheels and tyres before you buy. Look closely at this photograph and you'll see that both the tyre and the alloy are damaged and need replacing. At the very least, use this is a haggling tool. (Author)

◣ The interior of any smart is generally hard wearing – able to take plenty of use and even a bit of abuse. Early city-coupé interiors were the funkiest, thanks to their bright colours. This 2004 fortwo looks sombre by comparison. (Author)

This doesn't mean you shouldn't be on the lookout for panel damage when checking out a smart to buy, however. Many city-coupés and fortwos feature scratches and grazes, particularly around the protruding front and rear wheel-arches. Use this as a haggling tool when negotiating your purchase price, and you could end up with more of a bargain than you first thought. Check out the cost of any replacement panels you're likely to need though, before you start the negotiating process.

While on the subject of cosmetics, it's also important to pay attention to a smart's wheels – whether they're the plain steel rims of an early city-coupé smart&pure or the eye-catching alloys of a later fortwo. The former are very bland and uninspiring, especially when they're suffering from surface rust and looking a bit forlorn. The latter too can suffer from contact with kerbsides when parking. During your inspection of any smart, check out the condition of each wheel and be on the lookout for unsightly damage; putting it right will involve some expense, so don't be afraid to suggest this should be taken into account with the purchase price.

Inside a smart, things are generally very

hard-wearing and robust. Most of the materials used are of good quality, and it is unusual to see even high-mileage early city-coupés with completely wrecked interiors. Even so, it pays to look carefully for signs of wear and tear or obvious damage; again, this is sometimes reflected in the asking price, so you need to be realistic about what you're paying.

In reality though, these are the standard kind of warning signs that potential buyers of any used small car should be aware of. The good news is that, compared with some of the similarly priced second-hand competition, a used smart can take quite a battering before it really starts to suffer. These are robust, well built and seriously durable little cars which show other manufacturers that affordability doesn't have to mean a drop in standards.

Britain's *Auto Express* magazine summed it up when, during a used-car test in 2003, it suggested: 'You don't have to pay through the nose for Mercedes quality, and here's the car that proves it…'. Several years on from the launch of the first smart city-coupé, the quality is rarely in dispute, and for today's used car buyers, that's fantastic news.

RUNNING A SMART

Buying any new or used smart is a very individual process. From your exact choice of model and specification to your chosen method of buying the car in the first place, no two smart sales are ever the same. Well, what would you expect from Europe's most creative mass producer?

Once you have the smart of your choice parked on your driveway though, what's the ownership experience going to be like – and what's it likely to cost? While most smart buyers take pride in the fact their cars are produced by the same company as Mercedes-Benz and Maybach, they still demand sensible running costs. smart may be perceived as a prestige brand, but its cars still need to be frugal and cheap to run.

COSTS PER MILE

Potential buyers who have yet to catch on to the fact that the fortwo is the most technologically advanced car in its class can sometimes still be heard complaining that it's too expensive to buy. Certainly, in most of Europe there are cheaper cars available – all of them able to seat at least four people instead of the fortwo's twosome. But that's missing the point.

For a start, when you take a look at its exact specification, the fortwo is competitively priced. The entry-level pure model – with the standard 50bhp engine specified – costs broadly the same in most markets as the Chevrolet Matiz 1.0 SE, Daihatsu Charade 1.0 EL, Fiat Panda 1.1 Active, Ford Ka 1.3, Kia Picanto 1.1 LX, CityRover 1.4 Solo and SEAT Arosa 1.0 S. A handful of others (the Perodua Kelisa and Suzuki Alto included) undercut all these by as much as 10 per cent.

So the fortwo certainly isn't without competition, but how many of the aforementioned models come with such features as traction control, ABS, a turbocharger and a six-speed sequential semi-automatic gearbox? The simple answer is: none. What the fortwo lacks in seating capacity it more than makes up for in technical and electronic wizardry, making it by far the most advanced production city car anywhere in the world.

As for criticisms about the fortwo's lack of convenience, being just a two-seater ... well, isn't this exactly what the car was designed for in the first place? It is 2.5m (8ft 2in) long, which means it's by far the easiest car to park in any modern city, and how many people do you know who drive to work with more than one passenger on board anyway?

▷ **You might not think of a fortwo as the obvious company car of choice, but Britain's *Fleet Week* magazine saw the logic of it when, in 2003, they recognised its advantages through their Fleet Excellence Awards. (Author)**

▽ **The cheapest smart on sale – the fortwo pure – is also one of the most cost-effective cars on the road, thanks to running costs that significantly undercut models like the Ford Ka. (Author)**

△ **At just 2.5 metres long, a smart city-coupé or fortwo can be slotted into just about any parking space! Any disadvantages of its two-seater design are more than compensated for by its sheer versatility and manoeuvrability. (Author)**

Some of the criticism that has been levelled at the fortwo (and the city-coupé before it) over the years has been plain daft and what even the harshest of critics have failed to destroy is the little smart's achievements in terms of running costs.

Like so many motoring magazines throughout the world, Britain's *Auto Express* publishes guidelines as to what every new car currently available costs to run. In the case of the UK market, this is obviously measured in terms of 'pence per mile' – and it certainly makes for interesting reading.

Using figures for 2004, *Auto Express* states the cheapest smart fortwo pure (50bhp) comes in at a very competitive 25p per mile to run. On the other hand, a SEAT Arosa 1.0 S costs 27p; a Fiat Panda 1.1 Active costs 28p; both the Chevrolet Matiz 1.0 SE and Daihatsu Charade 1.0 EL each cost 29p,

and the Ford Ka 1.3 and CityRover 1.4 Solo come in at 31p per mile to run. Over three years and 30,000 miles, that can make a difference in running costs of £1,800 between the little fortwo and the entry-level Ford Ka – a considerable amount of money in the city car class.

So how are such figures worked out? Well, it's a combination of factors, including the initial purchase price, the likely depreciation levels, insurance costs, and fuel consumption, as well as the expense of servicing and repairs.

In depreciation alone, the fortwo is among the strongest performers in its class. The cheapest and least powerful fortwo pure offers – according to *Auto Express* – residuals of around 43 per cent after three years. This compares with figures of only 37 and 35 per cent respectively for the Ford Ka 1.3 and Daihatsu Charade 1.0 EL. Even taking into account the bigger discount that a Ford dealer is likely to offer with a Ka compared with what a fortwo buyer will be able to negotiate, there's no denying it's the smart that's top of the residuals league.

Elsewhere within the fortwo line-up, it's a similar story. The slowest-depreciating model is the pure cabriolet, which is claimed to still be worth a massive 67 per cent of its original list price after three years – a figure that no similarly priced car of any kind can hope to match. If depreciation is your main concern, running a brand-new fortwo pure cabriolet – and having a lot of fun in the process – could be the answer you've been looking for.

It's not just the fortwo though, that's economical to run; the roadster range is equally competitive within its class. For a start, the standard roadster is significantly cheaper to buy than the Mazda MX-5 1.6, MG TF 115 and Peugeot 206 CC 1.6S, although similarly priced to the Citroën C3 Pluriel 1.6 16v, Daihatsu Copen and Ford Streetka Luxury. Only the evergreen Fiat Barchetta has a usefully lower list price than the smart roadster in most European markets.

▲ Not only is every smart fun and funky in design, it is also commendably economical to run. It's true; there are plenty of independent statistics to back this up. (Author)

Things even up though, when you take into account the discounts that buyers of new MX-5s, TFs and 206s can usually agree through their dealers – the kind of reductions that most smart dealers simply won't entertain. Suddenly then, the roadster finds itself up against some very close competition when it comes to price.

Even so, in 2004 that didn't stop *Auto Express* giving the smart roadster a running cost of just 39p per mile – a figure that compares more than favourably with the Citroën C3 Pluriel 1.6 16v (46p), the Mazda MX-5 1.6, MG TF 115 and Ford Streetka Luxury (all 48p each), and the Peugeot 206 CC 1.6S at a whopping 51p. Over three years and 30,000 miles, that made a new smart roadster potentially £3,600 cheaper to run than the equivalent Peugeot 206 CC – a big saving by any standards.

Again, these were figures that had taken into account depreciation, fuel economy, servicing costs, insurance and just about every other aspect of running a new car. And time after time, it was the smart product that was coming out on top.

If depreciation is a big worry for you, then look no further than the fortwo cabrio. Amazingly, it could still be worth up to 67 per cent of its list price after three years on the road. (Author)

RELIABILITY AS STANDARD

Buyers nowadays don't just look for the least expensive running costs, though; they also demand a painless ownership experience. This means reliability has to come as standard – something that smart has always taken very seriously.

It's easy to look at the issue of reliability in a simplistic way. 'If it's owned by Mercedes it must be reliable', many people assume about smart. To a certain extent, that's true – but not automatically so. In various independent owners' surveys over the years, for example, the first-generation Mercedes-Benz A-class was criticised for its unreliability and poor quality – something that came as a shock to anybody who assumed the 'little Merc' was as beautifully built as its bigger brothers. With the smart range though, inbuilt quality and reliability are there in abundance.

Numerous independent surveys have confirmed this. Back in 2002, for example, *Top Gear* magazine conducted a survey of 37,000 motorists, quizzed on their experiences with reliability, running costs, driving enjoyment and treatment by dealers. A total of 120 different models from 33 manufacturers were covered. Not only did the smart city-coupé come third overall (praised by owners for its running costs, versatility

and reliability), but smart was voted second best manufacturer.

James Mills, deputy editor of *Top Gear* back then, was equally full of praise: 'This survey provided us with unbiased, spin-free information direct from those people who know their car best. smart might be tiny but owners have voted it brilliant to live with. Being voted best city car and taking third place overall, ahead of some seriously satisfying competition, is pretty good going…'

The following year, in 2003, Britain's *Which?* magazine – the publication of the Consumers' Association – published the results of a survey of more than 32,000 cars. Incredibly, and much to the embarrassment of smart's rivals, the results showed 100 per cent reliability for the city-coupé. Those owners who took part in the survey reported their cars had never broken down and were totally dependable.

Even now, several years on from the launch of the original-style city-coupé, only a tiny proportion of owners report any serious problems with their smarts. Pessimists who predicted at the outset that a small-engined, turbocharged city car couldn't hope to be reliable in the long term have been proved wrong. There are many high-mileage early smarts still happily giving good, reliable service on the roads of Europe. It's a tribute to the

It's not just city-coupés and fortwos that are economical to run; the roadster and roadster-coupé offer a healthy lead in the sports car sector. (Author)

original design and to the quality of materials used throughout the build process.

MORE SAVINGS

It is fascinating that the original city-coupé and current fortwo models offer extra, unexpected savings, too – ones that other vehicles in the city car class can't hope to compete with.

Much of Europe, for example, has introduced car park savings for owners of smart's smallest product. Because the car takes up only half the space of a larger vehicle, car park owners figured city-coupé and fortwo drivers deserved to pay less for their parking. Even the UK, traditionally slow to catch on to such new initiatives, has followed suit; back in 2003, major operator NCP announced a 25 per cent discount for owners of city-coupés using their car park in Portman Square, London. It was a small start, but hopefully

▷ **Look at the figures offered by *Auto Express* magazine in 2004 and you'll see the smart roadster was up to £3,600 cheaper to run over three years than a Peugeot 206 CC 1.6S. A sobering thought. (Author)**

its low carbon dioxide emissions, frugal fuel consumption, low insurance groupings, good residuals, and whole-life running costs.

BITS AND PIECES

No matter what model or age of smart you're running, another major bonus is the generally sensible pricing of any spare parts you're likely to need. Every smart centre throughout Europe carries comprehensive stocks of the most commonly used items. There is also a good spread of independent smart specialists in many countries, all boasting parts, accessories and service items at very competitive prices.

In the UK, companies like smart tune, smartstore, smarts-R-us and Euro Car Parts all claim to offer reasonable prices, excellent service

▽ **Wherever you intend having your smart maintained, repaired or uprated, make sure you choose either a smart centre or a reputable independent specialist. The best ones offer great service at very competitive costs. (Author)**

▲ **With Mercedes-style reliability on offer, your smart shouldn't need to visit your nearest smart centre for much more than routine servicing – even if your annual mileage is higher than average. (Author)**

it will encourage car park owners in other areas of the country to take up the challenge.

smart owners who enjoy travelling are well catered for, too. In 2001, for instance, Hoverspeed started offering discounts for city-coupé owners who use the company's high-speed cross-Channel ferry service, reclassifying the smart at 'motorcycle-plus-two-people' rate – a saving of up to 50 per cent. The following year, two more ferry operators followed suit: DFDS Seaways (covering Newcastle to Gothenberg, Kristiansand and Amsterdam, as well as Harwich to Esbjerg and Cuxhaven), and SeaFrance (on their Dover to Calais route) were also offering half-price deals for city-coupé drivers. If you own a city-coupé or a fortwo and you're planning any overseas trips, it's worth asking when you book whether there are any special deals for smart owners; the savings can be well worthwhile.

There are further savings in Britain too, for any city-coupé or fortwo owners running their smarts as company cars. With the oft-criticised Company Car Tax being based individually on a car's level of carbon dioxide emissions, the city-coupé and fortwo happily find themselves in the lowest tax bracket of all. Oh, and if you thought there wasn't a fleet market for the tiniest smart model, you'd better think again. *Fleet Week* magazine voted the city-coupé 'Best City Car' in its Fleet Excellence Awards 2003, praising it for

◁ **Every motoring survey of the last few years has confirmed the reliability of smart's rev-happy little three-cylinder engine. Members of the world's many smart clubs say the same, too. It's a dependable choice. (Author)**

and plenty of technical know-how. As with the classic car world, smart owners can certainly benefit from the experience and knowledge that independents like these can offer.

Much depends, of course, on who is going to be looking after your smart for you – your nearest smart centre, a local garage, or perhaps you'll be relying on your own DIY skills? Servicing and repair costs at smart centres are competitive and, even when a car's warranty expires, most smart owners choose to stay with the official dealer network. If a non-smart garage is carrying out work for you, or you're doing most of it yourself, it pays to shop around and compare the prices offered by the different specialists. Whether you're in need of an oil filter or a full new set of body panels, prices do vary. Get in touch with the companies direct (see Appendix B for contact details) and see what they can offer for your particular needs.

LIFE AT THE WHEEL

Having a car that doesn't cost a great deal to run, of course, is no good unless it's a pleasure to own – and to drive. Owners of the earliest city-coupés could have been forgiven for being annoyed by the lethargically slow gearchange, for example, but anybody lucky enough to drive a later city-coupé, current fortwo, any roadster or even the latest forfour should have no such problems. The current extensive smart line-up has no weak links in its particular chain.

Even the most basic of the fortwo models is a pleasure to drive on an everyday basis. Power is increased over earlier examples, which aids acceleration and makes it easier to keep up with fast-flowing traffic, and, as already covered in Chapter Three, the transmission is a massive step forward from the original design.

The biggest drawback with the fortwo is the feature that everyone notices first: its two-seater layout. The whole point about the new Mercedes-developed city car in 1998 though, was that it was just that – a commuter machine capable of carrying the driver, one passenger and a healthy number of personal belongings. So, if you think it may be difficult to manage with just two seats in your cheap-and-cheerful city car, you're looking in the wrong place.

◁ With the cost of car parking being discounted for owners of city-coupés and fortwos in many parts of Europe, could our car parks of the future look like this? Time will tell. (Author)

test drive the new
forfour
at smart birmingham
0121 506 2360

▽ The city-coupé and fortwo may have just two seats on offer – but they also have plenty of space for a pair of burly six-footers, as well as enough room behind the seats for a whole week's shopping. How can that be inconvenient? (Author)

△ Designing a 'supermini' that's individual, attractive and as practical as any rival is no mean feat, but smart achieved all three with the new forfour of 2004. (Author)

WHAT THE PRESS SAID: RUNNING A FORFOUR

'Drive it, and the Merc parentage is clear: this is a serious little car. It takes a thoughtful course down the road, is stable on motorways and secure through bends. It feels weighty and solid. But if you want to jostle it through corners, the smart pulls a disapproving frown. The 1.5-litre engine is nicely lively, though it sounds a bit loudmouthed. The 1.1-litre version is like a new puppy that enthusiastically begs you to go flat out everywhere.'

The Independent (UK), March 2004

From idiosyncratic manufacturer of a single-model city car to respected creator of a whole range of premium models, smart has come a long way in just a few years. The sheer achievement of this shouldn't be underestimated; it's a motor industry tale that actually looks like having a happy ending. (Author)

The advantage of the layout, of course, is that (for a two-seater) the fortwo is incredibly spacious. There's genuine space for a couple of six-footers to stretch out in comfort, and there's enough room behind the seats to take a week's shopping. Most smart owners agree that is a far better compromise than trying to squeeze four seats into such a tiny space.

Such problems don't arise, of course, with the forfour, co-developed with Mitsubishi and offering all the practicality of any Ford Fiesta or Volkswagen Polo – but without the bland styling. Yes, even when you choose smart's four-seater offering, you need to be prepared for the looks and stares from passers-by. Like the diminutive fortwo, the forfour knows how to attract attention wherever it goes; so if you're the shy and retiring type who likes to blend in to the background, perhaps a smart product of any description isn't the car for you…

smart should be congratulated on designing a family car that's very different from the norm. From its two-tone TRIDION-enhanced external styling to its slightly wacky and typically adventurous interior, the forfour is a five-door hatchback that screams individualism at anyone close enough to hear.

Having said that, the forfour is also an extremely practical machine. There's decent space

for a family, enough luggage room for a few overnight bags, and so many useful gadgets and neat touches on board that you feel as though you're flying Club Class. More cup holders than you can shake a stick at; front seats that fold forward to make handy tables for anyone in the back; back seats that slide backwards and forwards for the ideal passenger/luggage compromise; wild, funky colours that most rival manufacturers wouldn't even dare contemplate – they're all part of what makes the forfour unique.

And yet, for those who prefer the mechanical side of things to be fairly straightforward, the forfour is the first smart to feature front-wheel drive and an engine where most people would put it… at the front. It is, insist smart's followers, the perfect car for those who want a balance between 'different' and 'normal', and who are we to argue?

There's no chance of anyone criticising the roadster and roadster-coupé for being too normal, of course. Like the fortwo, these three-cylinder turbocharged sportsters really know how to put the fun back into motoring. See the driving impressions and comments in Chapter Four for the whole story. Meanwhile though, don't confuse 'fun and sporty' with 'cramped and impractical'; far from it. You see, this pair of low-slung top-handling sports cars offer all the room you and your passenger are ever likely to need, with the bonus of enough luggage space for the odd dirty weekend. You couldn't tackle a pan-European touring holiday in a smart roadster – but that's not the intention, is it?

What comes across strongly, driving any of the current range of smart models, is just how easy they all are to live with, and not just easy, but cheap too. For what is constantly being trumpeted by DaimlerChrysler as a premium brand, the whole-life costs throughout the range are incredibly competitive, with some of the lowest depreciation levels in the business, getting things off to a flying start.

There's no reason why this won't continue with the formore SUV; smart has come too far in such a short space of time to jeopardise its reputation now. The company soon learned how to gain negative publicity – all of which seems a long time ago now. Thanks to strenuous efforts on the part of smart, aided by a buying public ready to forgive earlier errors, things have rarely looked better for the marque. Life with a smart has never been easier, or more fun.

▼ For all their fun and thrills, both the roadster and roadster-coupé offer the kind of practicality you wouldn't necessarily expect from a modern reinterpretation of the MG Midget concept. (smart UK)

COLOUR CHOICE

Since the launch of the smart brand, a wide range of different colours has been available. This is the basic array for 2004/05:

FORTWO

lite white

star blue metallic

scratch black

phat red

bay grey metallic

numeric blue

jack black

river silver metallic

stream green

BRABUS FORTWO

jack black

river silver metallic

ROADSTER/ROADSTER-COUPÉ

shine yellow

champagne remix metallic

spice red

glance grey metallic

star blue metallic

jack black

BODY PANEL CHOICE

The following body panel pattern options became available for the city-coupé for the 2003 model year, as part of the 'smart individual' range:

CITY-COUPÉ

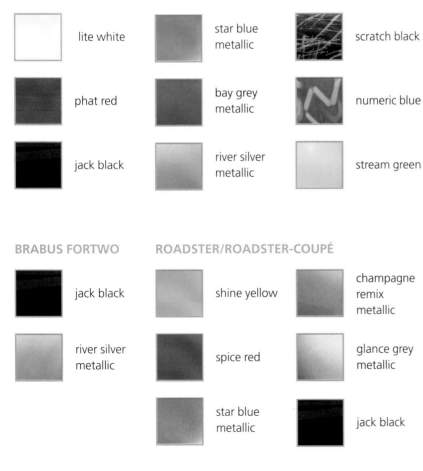

zebra stripes

tartan

cheetah spots

green lemonade bubbles

great white shark

superhero

London skyline

sheepdog

red tomatoes

sunlounger

CITY-COUPÉ (45BHP)

On sale:	October 1998 to March 2003
Engine:	599cc six-valve fuel-injected three-cylinder with turbocharger and intercooler
Max power:	45bhp @ 5,250rpm
Performance:	Max speed 84mph (135km/h) (electronically limited); 0–62mph (100km/h) 18.7sec
Economy:	57.6mpg (official combined figure)
Transmission:	Sequential semi-automatic six-speed gearbox
Clutch:	Single-plate dry
Front suspension:	Wishbone; MacPherson damper strut; anti-roll bar
Rear suspension:	De Dion suspension tube with central mount; wishbone; coil springs; telescopic shock absorbers; anti-roll bar
Brakes:	Front discs; rear drums; TRUST PLUS stability control (pre-2002); ABS
Steering:	Rack-and-pinion
Overall length:	2,500mm
Overall width:	1,515mm
Overall height:	1,549mm
Wheelbase:	1,812mm

CITY-COUPÉ (54BHP)

On sale:	October 1998 to March 2003
Engine:	599cc six-valve fuel-injected three-cylinder with turbocharger and intercooler
Max power:	54bhp @ 5,250rpm (61bhp in city-coupé pulse)
Performance:	Max speed 84mph (135km/h) (electronically limited); 0–62mph (100km/h) 16.8sec
Economy:	57.6mpg (official combined figure)
Transmission:	Sequential semi-automatic six-speed gearbox
Clutch:	Single-plate dry
Front suspension:	Wishbone; MacPherson damper strut; anti-roll bar
Rear suspension:	De Dion suspension tube with central mount; wishbone; coil springs; telescopic shock absorbers; anti-roll bar
Brakes:	Front discs; rear drums; TRUST PLUS stability control (pre-2002); ABS
Steering:	Rack-and-pinion
Overall length:	2,500mm
Overall width:	1,515mm
Overall height:	1,549mm
Wheelbase:	1,812mm

CITY-COUPÉ/FORTWO (50BHP)

On sale:	From March 2003
Engine:	698cc six-valve fuel-injected three-cylinder with turbocharger and intercooler
Max power:	50bhp @ 5,250rpm
Performance:	Max speed 84mph (135km/h) (electronically limited); 0–62mph (100km/h) 18.3sec
Economy:	47.9mpg (urban); 70.6mpg (extra urban); 60.1mpg (combined)
Transmission:	Sequential semi-automatic six-speed gearbox
Clutch:	Single-plate dry
Front suspension:	Wishbone; MacPherson damper strut; anti-roll bar
Rear suspension:	De Dion suspension tube with central mount; wishbone; coil springs; telescopic shock absorbers; anti-roll bar
Brakes:	Front discs; rear drums; ESP; EBD; ABS
Steering:	Rack-and-pinion; power-assistance at extra cost
Overall length:	2,500mm
Overall width:	1,515mm
Overall height:	1,549mm
Wheelbase:	1,812mm

CITY-CABRIO (ALL MODELS)

On sale (UK):	From 2001
Engines:	599cc and 698cc six-valve fuel-injected three-cylinder with turbocharger and intercooler

NB: Figures are generally the same as for city-coupé; similar upgrades to city-coupé during model's life; engine outputs are in-line with relevant city-coupé derivatives.

CITY-COUPÉ/FORTWO (61BHP)

On sale:	From March 2003	Front suspension:	Wishbone; MacPherson damper strut; anti-roll bar
Engine:	698cc six-valve fuel-injected three-cylinder with turbocharger and intercooler	Rear suspension:	De Dion suspension tube with central mount; wishbone; coil springs; telescopic shock absorbers; anti-roll bar
Max power:	61bhp @ 5,250rpm		
Performance:	Max speed 84mph (135km/h) (electronically limited); 0–62mph (100km/h) 15.5 secs	Brakes:	Front discs; rear drums; ESP; EBD; ABS
Economy:	47.9mpg (urban); 70.6mpg (extra urban); 60.1mpg (combined)	Steering:	Rack-and-pinion; power-assistance at extra cost
		Overall length:	2,500mm
		Overall width:	1,515mm
Transmission:	Sequential semi-automatic six-speed gearbox	Overall height:	1,549mm
		Wheelbase:	1,812mm
Clutch:	Single-plate dry		

CITY-COUPÉ/FORTWO CDI

On sale:	From 2000 (not available in UK)	Rear suspension:	De Dion suspension tube with central mount; wishbone; coil springs; telescopic shock absorbers; anti-roll bar
Engine:	799cc six-valve fuel-injected three-cylinder common-rail turbo-diesel		
Max power:	40bhp @ 4,200rpm	Brakes:	Front discs; rear drums; ESP; EBD; ABS
Performance:	Max speed 84mph (135km/h) (electronically limited); 0–62mph (100km/h) 20.8sec	Steering:	Rack-and-pinion; power-assistance at extra cost
Economy:	70–90mpg (owners' average)	Overall length:	2,500mm
Transmission:	Sequential semi-automatic six-speed gearbox	Overall width:	1,515mm
		Overall height:	1,549mm
Clutch:	Single-plate dry	Wheelbase:	1,812mm
Front suspension:	Wishbone; MacPherson damper strut; anti-roll bar		

BRABUS CITY-COUPÉ/FORTWO

On sale:	From 2002	Front suspension:	Wishbone; MacPherson damper strut; anti-roll bar
Engine:	698cc six-valve fuel-injected three-cylinder with turbocharger and intercooler	Rear suspension:	De Dion suspension tube with central mount; wishbone; coil springs; telescopic shock absorbers; anti-roll bar
Max power:	74bhp @ 5,250rpm		
Performance:	Max speed 94mph (151km/h); 0–62mph (100km/h) 12.3sec	Brakes:	Front discs; rear drums; ESP; EBD; ABS
Economy:	43.5mpg (urban); 61.4mpg (extra urban); 53.3mpg (combined)	Steering:	Rack-and-pinion
		Overall length:	2,500mm
Transmission:	Sequential semi-automatic six-speed gearbox	Overall width:	1,515mm (BRABUS cabrio: 1,537mm)
Clutch:	Single-plate dry	Overall height:	1,549mm
		Wheelbase:	1,812mm

CROSSBLADE

On sale:	From February 2002	Front suspension:	Wishbone; MacPherson damper strut; anti-roll bar
Engine:	599cc six-valve fuel-injected three-cylinder with turbocharger and intercooler	Rear suspension:	De Dion suspension tube with central mount; wishbone; coil springs; telescopic shock absorbers; anti-roll bar
Max power:	70bhp @ 5,470rpm		
Performance:	Max speed 85mph (137km/h) (electronically limited); 0–62mph (100km/h) 17.0sec	Brakes:	Front discs; rear drums; EBD; ABS
Economy:	45.6mpg (urban); 53.3mpg (extra urban); 49.6mpg (combined)	Steering:	Rack-and-pinion
		Overall length:	2,622mm
		Overall width:	1,618mm
Transmission:	Sequential semi-automatic six-speed gearbox	Overall height:	1,508mm
		Wheelbase:	1,812mm
Clutch:	Single-plate dry		

ROADSTER

On sale:	From April 2003	Front suspension:	Wishbone; MacPherson strut; stabiliser
Engine:	698cc six-valve fuel-injected three-cylinder with turbocharger and intercooler	Rear suspension:	De Dion suspension tube with central mount; wishbone; coil springs; telescopic shock absorbers
Max power:	80bhp @ 5,250rpm		
Performance:	Max speed 109mph (175km/h); 0–62mph (100km/h) 10.9sec	Brakes:	Front discs; rear drums; ESP; ABS
Economy:	44.8mpg (urban); 65.7mpg (extra urban); 55.4mpg (combined)	Steering:	Rack-and-pinion with electric power steering
Transmission:	Sequential semi-automatic six-speed gearbox	Overall length:	3,427mm
		Overall width:	1,615mm
Clutch:	Single-plate dry	Overall height:	1,192mm
		Wheelbase:	2,360mm

ROADSTER-COUPÉ

On sale:	From April 2003	Front suspension:	Wishbone; MacPherson strut; stabiliser
Engine:	698cc six-valve fuel-injected three-cylinder with turbocharger and intercooler	Rear suspension:	De Dion suspension tube with central mount; wishbone; coil springs; telescopic shock absorbers
Max power:	80bhp @ 5,250rpm		
Performance:	Max speed 113mph 182km/h); 0–62mph (100km/h) 11.2sec	Brakes:	Front discs; rear drums; ESP; ABS
Economy:	44.1mpg (urban); 65.7mpg (extra urban); 55.4mpg (combined)	Steering:	Rack-and-pinion with electric power steering
Transmission:	Sequential semi-automatic six-speed gearbox	Overall length:	3,427mm
		Overall width:	1,615mm
Clutch:	Single-plate dry	Overall height:	1,192mm
		Wheelbase:	2,360mm

BRABUS ROADSTER-COUPÉ

On sale:	From 2004
Engine:	698cc six-valve fuel-injected three-cylinder with turbocharger and intercooler
Max power:	101bhp @ 5,250rpm
Performance:	Max speed 119mph (191km/h) (roadster: 122mph/196km/h); 0–62mph (100km/h) 9.8sec
Economy:	42.8mpg (urban); 61.4mpg (extra urban); 53.3mpg (combined)
Transmission:	Sequential semi-automatic six-speed gearbox
Clutch:	Single-plate dry
Front suspension:	Wishbone; MacPherson strut; stabiliser
Rear suspension:	De Dion suspension tube with central mount; wishbone; coil springs; telescopic shock absorbers
Brakes:	Front discs; rear drums; ESP; ABS
Steering:	Rack-and-pinion with electric power steering
Overall length:	3,427mm
Overall width:	1,615mm
Overall height:	1,190mm
Wheelbase:	2,360mm

FORFOUR 1.1

On sale:	From 2004
Engine:	1,124cc in-line three-cylinder petrol
Max power:	75bhp @ 5,800rpm
Performance:	Max speed 103mph; 0–62mph 13.4 secs
Economy:	40.4mpg (urban); 61.4mpg (extra urban); 51.4mpg (combined)
Transmission:	Five-speed manual/six-speed semi-automatic sequential
Clutch:	Single-plate dry clutch
Suspension:	MacPherson struts; coil springs; anti-roll bar
Brakes:	Discs all round; Electronic Stability Program; ABS
Steering:	Rack and pinion with electric power steering
Overall length:	3,752mm
Overall width:	1,684mm
Overall height:	1,450mm
Wheelbase:	2,500mm

FORFOUR 1.3

On sale:	From 2004
Engine:	1,332cc in-line four-cylinder petrol
Max power:	95bhp @ 5,900rpm
Performance:	Max speed 112mph; 0–62mph 10.8 secs
Economy:	38.2mpg (urban); 58.9mpg (extra urban); 48.7mpg (combined)
Transmission:	Five-speed manual/six-speed semi-automatic sequential
Clutch:	Single-plate dry clutch
Suspension:	MacPherson struts; coil springs; anti-roll bar
Brakes:	Discs all round; Electronic Stability Program; ABS
Steering:	Rack and pinion with electric power steering
Overall length:	3,752mm
Overall width:	1,684mm
Overall height:	1,450mm
Wheelbase:	2,500mm

FORFOUR 1.5

On sale:	From 2004	Clutch:	Single-plate dry clutch
Engine:	1,499cc in-line four-cylinder petrol	Suspension:	MacPherson struts; coil springs; anti-roll bar
Max power:	109bhp @ 5,900rpm	Brakes:	Discs all round; Electronic Stability Program; ABS
Performance:	Max speed 118mph; 0–62mph 9.8 secs	Steering:	Rack and pinion with electric power steering
Economy:	36.2mpg (urban); 55.4mpg (extra urban); 46.3mpg (combined)	Overall length:	3,752mm
		Overall width:	1,684mm
Transmission:	Five-speed manual/six-speed semi-automatic sequential	Overall height:	1,450mm
		Wheelbase:	2,500mm

FORFOUR 1.5 CDI (68BHP)

On sale:	From 2004	Clutch:	Single-plate dry clutch
Engine:	1,493cc in-line three-cylinder common rail direct-injection diesel	Suspension:	MacPherson struts; coil springs; anti-roll bar
Max power:	68bhp @ 4,000rpm	Brakes:	Discs all round; Electronic Stability Program; ABS
Performance:	Max speed 99mph; 0–62mph 13.9 secs	Steering:	Rack and pinion with electric power steering
Economy:	47.9mpg (urban); 72.4mpg (extra urban); 61.4mpg (combined)	Overall length:	3,752mm
		Overall width:	1,684mm
Transmission:	Five-speed manual/six-speed semi-automatic sequential	Overall height:	1,450mm
		Wheelbase:	2,500mm

FORFOUR 1.5 CDI (95BHP)

On sale:	From 2004	Clutch:	Single-plate dry clutch
Engine:	1,493cc in-line three-cylinder common rail direct-injection diesel	Suspension:	MacPherson struts; coil springs; anti-roll bar
Max power:	95bhp @ 4,000rpm	Brakes:	Discs all round; Electronic Stability Program; ABS
Performance:	Max speed 112mph; 0–62mph 10.5 secs	Steering:	Rack and pinion with electric power steering
Economy:	47.9mpg (urban); 72.4mpg (extra urban); 61.4mpg (combined)	Overall length:	3,752mm
		Overall width:	1,684mm
		Overall height:	1,450mm
Transmission:	Five-speed manual/six-speed semi-automatic sequential	Wheelbase:	2,500mm

APPENDIX B
SPECIALISTS, CLUBS AND CONTACTS

SPECIALISTS

smartimes magazine
9 Downlands Road, Winchester SO22 4ET,
England
Tel: +44 (0)1962 626585
Website: www.smartimes.co.uk
A quarterly magazine specifically for smart
owners, available by subscription only. Can be
delivered anywhere in the world. Subscriptions
can be ordered via thesmartclub, funkysmart or
through the magazine's own website.

smarts-R-us Ltd
Phoenix Farm Car Centre, Arnold Lane, Gedling,
Nottingham NG4 4HF, England
Tel: +44 (0)115 956 7896 (accessories) or +44
(0)115 961 1000 (car sales)
Website: www.smartsrus.com
Market-leading suppliers of accessories, perfor-
mance upgrades, body kits and uprated smarts.
Vast range available; check the website for the
latest information.

smart tune
Tel: 0870 880 3430 (head office), 0870 880 3430
(UK orders) or +44 (0)870 880 3432 (interna-
tional orders)
Website: www.smarttune.co.uk
E-mail: sales@smarttune.co.uk
Large stocks of smart parts, accessories and
upgrades for all models. Expert advice and sup-
port always available.

smart store
Tyrrell Automotive, Vitalograph Business Park,
Maids Moreton, Buckinghamshire MK18 1SW,

England
Tel: +44 (0)870 600 1828
Website: www.smartstore.co.uk
E-mail: info@smartstore.co.uk
Car sales, accessories and custom-made 'busi-
ness packages' for promotional purposes.

cambridge smart cars
3–5 Breckenwood Road, Fulbourn, Cambridge
CB1 5DQ, England
Tel: +44 (0)1223 881517
Website: www.cambridgesmartcars.co.uk
E-mail: cambridge.smartcars@virgin.net
Independent importers of left- and right-hand
drive smart fortwos and retailers of used smarts;
accessories and parts also in stock.

Chipped smart
Website: www.chipped-smart.co.uk
E-mail: info@chipped-smart.co.uk
A British company specialising in remapping and
performance upgrades for all smart models.

Euro Sports Cars
Tel: +44 (0)1753 648064
Website: www.euro-sportscars.com
E-mail: info@euro-sportscars.com
Digi-tec engine upgrades for all smart models;
UK supplier of Digi-tec Limited Edition smart
roadster.

smart trailer
Website: www.smarttrailer.co.uk
E-mail: info@smarttrailer.co.uk
A British website offering tow bars and specially
designed trailers for smarts.

t1ny.com
Tel: +44 (0)7740 342899
Website: www.t1ny.com
Specialists in and enthusiasts of modified smarts,
with a wide range of upgrades.

SW-Exclusive
Karosseriedesign & Leistungsoptimierung GmbH,
Mainzer Strasse 97, 65189 Wiesbaden, Germany
Tel: +49 (0)6112 3 67 19 5.
Website: www.sw-exclusive.de
E-mail: kontakt@swexclusive.de
Suppliers of modified smarts of all types, as well
as a range of special modifications and upgrades.

Opera Design
Kassbohrerstrabe 3, 88471 Laupheim, Germany
Tel: +49 (0)7392 9 73 23 00
Website: www.opera-design.de
E-mail: info@opera-design.de
Designers and manufacturers of body kits and
styling accessories for smarts; tuning upgrades
and wheel/tyre combinations also available.

parts4smarts
Tel: +49 (0)6131 6 90 02 20
Website: www.parts4smarts.de
E-mail: kontakt@parts4smarts.de
German-based specialists in parts, accessories
and upgrades for all smart models.

smartspeed
Website: www.smartspeed.de
E-mail: kontakt@smartspeed.de
German-based tuning and modifying company
specialising in smarts.

Lumma Tuning
Weinstetter Strasse, D-72474 Winterlingen,
Germany
Tel: +49 (0)7577 3313
Website: www.lumma-tuning.de
E-mail: info@lumma-tuning.de
Suppliers of 'body styling programs' for several
marques, including smart.

Clever Trailer
Hans Grunig, Birkenweg 18, CH-3250 Lyss,
Switzerland
Tel: +41 (0)76 385 07 42
Website: www.clevertrailer.ch
E-mail: clevertrailer@gmx.ch
Manufacturers of a glassfibre trailer specially
designed for towing behind the smart city-coupé
and fortwo.

Fede Racing
Via Cerzeto 11, 00173 Roma, Italy
Tel: 06/7234972
Website: www.federacing.it
Italian-based tuning company offering perfor-
mance upgrades for smarts.

smart tuning
Via Martiri della Liberta, 26-20077 Melegnano,
Milan, Italy
Website: www.smart-tuning.it
E-mail: info@smart-tuning.it
Italian company offering tuned smarts, power
upgrades and accessories.

SmartBil
Website: www.smartbil.info.se
Swedish-based supplier of smart parts, accessories and upgrades offering a Europe-wide service with free delivery.

CLUBS

smart owners tend to be computer-savvy and
enjoy the Internet. That's why most of the world's
smart clubs tend to be website-based, with
members joining online and receiving updates
and newsletters (where applicable) the same way.
Below is a selection of the best smart clubs we
came across during research for this book:

UNITED KINGDOM
www.thesmartclub.co.uk
www.funkysmart.co.uk
www.northeastsmarts.co.uk
www.midlandsmarts.co.uk
www.sussexsmarts.co.uk
www.smart.gb.com
www.smart-drivers.co.uk
www.smartclub-uk.com

GERMANY
www.smart-club.de
www.smart-club.rheinland.de
www.smart-club-sh.de
www.smart-club-nds.de
www.smart-club-berlin.de
www.smart-club-nordhessen.de
www.smartclub-vogtland.de
www.smart-driver.de
www.smart-friends.de
www.smart-forum.de
www.smartaholics.de
www.smart-owl.de
www.smart-in.de
www.smartandsmile.de
www.smartroadster-club.de
www.smart-roadster-board.de

SWITZERLAND
www.smartclub.ch
www.smartmembers.ch
www.clubsmart.ch

ITALY
www.eurosmartclub.com
www.neurosmart.it
www.smartandfurious.it

SPAIN
www.geocities.com/smartclubes

GREECE
www.smartmania.gr

SWEDEN
www.smartfan.nu

THE NETHERLANDS
www.smart-club.nl

AUSTRIA
www.smart-club.at
www.sccv.at

BELGIUM
www.smart-club.be

MEXICO
http://smartclub.2ya.com

AUSTRALIA
www.smartclubaustralia.com

TAIWAN
www.smart-club.com.tw

FUN AND USEFUL WEBSITES
The following websites have been set up by
smart owners and fanatics. They're great fun, as
well as being an effective way of keeping in
touch with other owners.

www.smartcar-owner.co.uk
www.smarthell.co.uk
www.smartowner.co.uk
www.thexblade.co.uk
www.worldofsmart.co.uk
www.smartmaniacs.co.uk
www.mccsmart.com
www.nordkap.ch
www.smartcars-funsite.nl
www.mysmart.tk
www.smart-welt.de
www.smart-ontour.com
www.smart-top100.de.vu
www.rhein-main-smarties.de
www.smart-essen.de
www.world-of-smart.de
www.smartplanet.de
www.berlin-tuning.com
http://goldklus.tk

GLOBAL SMART
To find out more about the smart brand and its
products in any of the countries in which it is represented, log on to www.smart.com and select
your country of choice. You will then be directed
to the company's official website specific to your
market.

INDEX